Practical Scent Dog Training

by
Lue Button

Illustrations by
Susan Henke

Alpine
PUBLICATIONS
Loveland, Colorado 80537

Library of Congress Cataloging-in-Publication Data

Button, Lue. 1929–
    Practical scent dog training / by Lue Button : illustrations by
Susan Henke.
        p.   cm.
    Includes bibliographical references.
    ISBN 0-931866-47-2
    1. Tracking Dogs--Training.   I. Title.   II. Title: Scent dog training.
SF428.75.886 1990
636.7'0886--dc20   90-184
                                                                                             CIP

This book is available at special quantity discounts for breeders and for club promotions, premiums, or educational use. Write for details.

        4 5 6 7 8 9 0

Cover design: Joan Harris

Printed in the United States of America.

CONTENTS

Dedication

To the Weimaraners Von Knopf for making this book possible:

Rudi der Riedlich, who taught me to pay attention
Starlit Banner, who started me in Tracking
Newbury Duke, who showed me what the books never told
Rudi der Reger, who introduced me to Search & Rescue
Simon, who taught me a new mode of persistence
Laser, who rescued the scent objects the others missed
Fujiyama, who changed my mind about bitches in search work
and all the others I hope are yet to come.

I. A TRAINED SCENT DOG IS A JOY FOREVER

Margaret had dropped her keys, somewhere in the snow-covered parking lot. She was numb with cold, pushing the heavy supermarket cart, and her purse, swinging from her shoulder, had fallen open. But a cheerful "yip" from the front seat told her that help was waiting. Margaret banked the cart wheels with snow, reached inside, and snapped the lead on Trinket, her little terrier. "Go find!" she said, pointing to the ground. Trinket scurried over the ruts, backtracking the rapidly filling footprints. Down the line of cars, across the entrance drive, up the curb--and then a sudden turnabout. The little paws scraped madly, sending up a shower of snow. The nose dropped, the mouth darted in, and the dog pranced back to Margaret to deposit the missing keys proudly in her hand.

Jim groped frantically in the grass. His glasses must be here! He remembered laying them on a rock just before he drank from the stream. As it was, Jim's son-in-law kept reminding him how much they had cost. And Jim was almost blind without them. A cold nose touched his cheek. Of course! Jenny! He scented her on the empty case from his pocket. A rush of eager feet, a splash, a joyful yelp, and the glasses were pressed into his hand. He put them on carefully and looked around. Not even the mountain peaks seemed familiar. But that was no problem. He patted the smooth head. "Find the car, Jenny," he said. "Take me to the car."

Phyllis was changing the baby, again. She was tired, oh, so tired. And two-year-old Allison was playing happily on the grass in front of the summer cabin. Or was she? Phyllis snapped alert. The clearing was empty. The surrounding woods were still. Phyllis called to Buck where he lay on the porch. "Find her, Buck. Find Allie." The dog shook himself awake, circled nose-down where the child had dropped her doll, then lined out through the trees. Phyllis stumbled after him, clutching the baby in her arms. On and on, over hill and through thickets; she could hear Buck moving in the brush. Then the sound stopped. She burst out onto the shoulder of the highway--to see Buck holding Allie's jacket firmly in his teeth, dragging her back from the road.

These were ordinary people, and their dogs were ordinary dogs. The fact that the dogs were trained to use scenting skills for their owners made the difference between inconvenience or possible tragedy and a happy outcome. They took up scent training casually, with no thought of ever having to use it. Margaret entered Trinket in a tracking class just because she wanted to continue working with her dog after basic obedience. Jim had thought his grandson should have a dog, but when everyone else was at school or work, the two of them had to do something together. Phyllis rescued Buck from the pound and trained him from a book she'd found in the college library because she thought it would be "neat" to have a scent dog; she'd forgotten all about it in the four years since she graduated and got married.

At the other extreme are the professionals: the police bloodhound handlers, the ski patrollers with their avalanche dogs, the many search and rescue (SAR) teams throughout the country. Scenting dogs are used to detect smuggled drugs, to find weapons in school children's lockers, to locate breaks in gas lines, and even to prospect for valuable metal deposits. These are the applications that make headlines, leading people to believe there is some mystique about scent training. It must be very difficult.

Not so! Scent work is the easiest form of dog training. Because it is usually done (or at least begun) on lead, you can do it anywhere, even in the heart of the city. You can do it from a wheelchair in your apartment. You can do it by yourself or with friends. All you need to get started is a dog, a harness, and an open mind. The rewards are great. No activity builds a closer understanding between dog and man, or a stronger mutual respect. Almost every dog loves scent work, whether because he is getting a chance to do what he's best at or because his beloved person is giving him total attention, only the dogs can tell. For the handler, there is the intellectual excitement of watching a skill unfold, the pride of seeing your own dog accomplish unbelievable things. And you will feel more secure knowing that, in emergencies, help is always at your side.

How easy is it? Many dogs start doing scent work on their own, with no training at all. Twenty years ago, my first Weimaraner tumbled to the fact that I needed two things to leave for work--my car keys and my security badge. Because he never wanted me to go to work, he would steal my badge or keyring and bury it in the garden.

I also was keeping a young puppy, Duke, for a friend. Duke was very devoted to me and got worried if I was distressed. The first time may have been an accident, but one morning while I was scolding Rudi, Duke all on his own dug up my keys and brought them to me. The praise I gave him that morning was all the training he ever had; from that day, I would say, "Find my keys," or "Find my badge," and Duke would do it, snuffling through the flowerbeds until he found where Rudi had dug. At the time I had no idea of training a dog to scent. I was just happy to find things I needed promptly.

Years later my confidence in this naive approach was confirmed when I read (Davis, p. 87) "Bear in mind that you are not teaching the dog to track.

You are training him to follow a specific trail* on your command...." That is the key to all scent work. You don't teach the dog to do it; you teach him to do it **for you**. Every puppy starts using his nose before his eyes open, to find his milk and the life-giving warmth generated by his mother. He sniffs his way through the mass of littermates to the food dish when weaning begins. On his first ventures outside, he scents where his mother and siblings have gone when he falls behind, and can even backtrack himself to your door. If you let him out after taking his brother for a walk, he will follow your tracks to learn what you did with that other dog. The only dog that does not scent (barring a physical handicap) is one raised to believe his nose was useless or always got him in trouble; in other words, he was **taught** not to.

Is it hard to get the dog to work on command? Sometimes. It depends on the dog's inborn temperament, his previous experience, and your attitude. We must remember, however, that dogs have made their living for thousands of years by pleasing their humans and that dogs are pack animals whose natural behavior is to work with a leader they respect. Most dogs happily do what you want, if you can show them what that is ar convince them it's worth doing.

Scent work leans heavily on mutual respect. If you cannot face the fact that this "dumb animal" has a sense several million times more acute than yours and knows instinctively more about using it than you will ever learn, you may find this training frustrating rather than enjoyable. Worse, a dominant dog will rebel against being restrained from using his best judgment and a submissive dog will be spoiled for practical work because he will look to you rather than use his nose. But before you abandon the idea of scent training, scan Chapter II and judge if a dog you can depend on is not more appealing than one that depends wholly on you.

How do you know what your dog is doing—whether he is scenting at all? By watching him. Every dog has its own body language, its individual way of working, its unique manner of communicating. By close observation, you can learn your dog's language. You will not only understand what your dog is doing but how he feels about it: whether he is sure of the trail or questing hopefully, and what conditions the trail has undergone since your subject passed this way. Your dog will have different signs for a passing rabbit track, a casual picnicker crossing the trail, or the presence of danger, and he will show increasing urgency if the subject is ill or injured. No book, including this one, can tell you how to "read" your dog; it can only suggest some common signs and how they appear in different types of dog.

---

* Davis uses "trail" to denote the more or less continuous series of scent traces which another writer might call a "track"--probably because "track" might be taken to mean a visual trace, such as a footprint.

Can all dogs do scent work, whether purebred or crossbred? Definitely. All dogs have a scent capability far surpassing a human's; temperament rather than pedigree is most likely to affect success. The Bloodhound and some of the sporting dogs have been bred for scent work over many years, so these dogs may in general prove more talented, but every dog has enough ability to be worth training. A young puppy is probably the easiest to start; but the older dog that already has scent experience under various conditions may develop a finished skill faster. A dominant dog should not be avoided; although possibly harder to train, such a dog may have more endurance when conditions get rough, more determination to follow the trail to the end, and more imagination in pursuit of the goal. A submissive dog can succeed, but he must be carefully trained for independence and confidence.

Dominant dog.

Submissive dog.

Is extensive reading a good idea? Shouldn't the various theories be studied? It is probably better to do your reading after you train your first scent dog. The references listed in the Bibliography contain much interesting material, but any theory which is directly controverted by something you have seen your own dog do should be accepted guardedly, if at all. For example, you will read that all individual human scent is gone after two hours--yet your dog is confused in practice by a conflicting trail the same tracklayer made the previous week and not by tracks of a strange hiker who crossed the trail that morning. When experience contradicts theory, go with experience.

Studying others' experiments, watch out for conclusions that may be artifacts of the dogs' previous training. For example, we read that dogs coming perpendicularly onto a track are apt to turn right consistently or left consistently regardless of which way the tracklayer had gone--does this mean the dogs cannot distinguish track direction, or were the first tracks they ran double- and triple-laid, back and forth over the same path, so that the dogs learned the direction of the track was not significant? When you start setting up your own experiments, beware of similar pitfalls.

Remember that many well-trained dogs have been produced by people who never read a book; they relied on their own common sense. In the long run, that is what you must do. Cultivate your powers of observation, then watch your dog. Try to understand everything your dog did (it's not always easy) and don't forget to consider possible alternate explanations. Then go confidently forward. Keep your training lively, keep it spontaneous. Don't bore your dog, or yourself. Above all, have fun.

II. WE'RE BOTH IN THIS TOGETHER

To have any practical use, scent work with your dog must be a partnership. A dog may have a fine nose, but if he cannot or will not communicate what his nose is telling him, his sense of smell is his personal toy and no information is conveyed to his handler. Fortunately, because dogs are pack animals, letting their packmates know what they have found is instinctive-- whether it be to help with the hunt or to share the spoils. The dog will give signals; the handler's job is to "read" them.

How simple things would be if dogs could speak our language! But they obviously cannot, so we must learn to understand theirs and give them a chance to learn which of their signals we are able to comprehend. For example, one of my dogs that has been running along the creek will come in and put his head on my shoulder with the long hair on his neck pressed against my cheek, close to my nose. He will do this with another dog, both standing nose to neck, and the other dog will understand what he found in his travels. Sometimes I do, too--if he was chasing a skunk or plunging through the cattails after a duck--but more often my sense of smell isn't up to the task and I have to take him to the door and say, "Show me." The puppies are often frustrated that I am so dense; it takes them several months to learn that I actually am "scent-deaf" compared to them and am not just refusing to pay attention.

The dog can't learn your limitations if he lives out in the kennel while you live in the house, nor can he develop ways to communicate which you can understand. All he can do is howl, and the neighbors will probably make you shut him up before you learn to distinguish which howl means there's a dangerous vehicle coming around the hill, which one means the neighbor's cat is after the pigeons, which one means the coyotes are talking over on the ridge, which one means he's just lonely.

So, the scent dog must live in the house, and you must give him as much attention as you would a business partner. You are the managing partner: you decide whom or what to search for, equip the partnership, transport the team, choose the starting point, and write the reports afterward. Therefore, the main responsibility for communicating is yours.

Start with your partner's obvious needs. To get outside, does he grab at your clothes and pull you toward the door, bring you his lead, scratch at the door frame, or sit by the door and look mournful? If his water pan is dry, does he bring it to you (possibly bang it on the refrigerator door), stand by you panting ostentatiously, or merely howl? Each dog has his own signs, and by watching him you will learn what they are.

```
IMPORTANT: NEVER PUNISH YOUR DOG FOR COMMUNICATING.
```

You may, however, substitute one sign for another. If you answer the dog's first signal, you may never see his insistent, obnoxious one. Give him water when he picks up the empty pan and he won't have a chance to bang it on the refrigerator. Tell him, "Wait" when he starts for the door to let him know you got the message, then open it promptly so that he hasn't time to scratch the glass. At his first bark when a car turns in the driveway, imme- diately say, "Thank you" and pet him to convey that you're grateful for the warning but that's enough; if he still seems worried, take him with you on lead to answer the door. This tells him you have the situation well in hand. Simply yelling "Shut up!" implies either that you didn't understand he was cautioning you or else that you think he's too stupid to know danger when he senses it. Either way, his natural reaction is to insist, to bark louder.

Do take your dog's signals seriously. Sometimes what he considers a grave threat may be inconsequential to you, but every so often you'll be glad you listened. One morning when Rudi and I were tracking in the National Forest, he froze, then slunk back to me and pressed against my legs, trying to force me away from the tracks I saw in the mud. I urged him on; he blocked me from moving forward. Then a wisp of breeze from the thicket just ahead brought me a raw, rough scent like that of a poorly kept pigpen. Bear! The side trail Rudi wanted me to take suddenly seemed very attractive! Detouring the thicket, we regained the track on the other side of the ridge.

So from the time you first bring your dog home, look and listen--and respond. Give your dog positive feedback, let him know you have understood. As you start formal training, watch for every sound, sniff, movement, posture, even change of pace your dog makes.

First, you need to recognize what is normal working behavior for your dog at whatever skill you are learning. Each dog will be different. In the lesson plans, some signs to watch for are mentioned; but your dog will doubtless have others that are unique to him. (This, by the way, is one reason a stranger can't walk in and handle your dog effectively on a search; he hasn't learned to read him. It also raises a question of how some criteria for judging a search dog candidate should be interpreted. "Dog must show a readable alert" is downright unfair if it means the **evaluators**, supposedly unknown to dog and handler, should be able to read the alert.)

Your preliminary observations around home should tell you when your dog is unable to work because of thirst or other physical need. Teach the dog to drink from your canteen, unless you carry a special cup for him. Do not think, because your dog goes to relieve himself shortly after starting, that he is unwilling to work or is not serious about the task--in fact, the more excited the dog becomes about searching and the more eagerly he looks forward to getting started, the more apt he is to feel a call of nature. It is interesting that most dogs will do this off to one side of the trail or track, as if trying not to interfere with the subject's scent.

Once you get the habit of really noticing your dog, it becomes automatic, and you can start noticing the environment in which you work. Especially at first, such factors as temperature, humidity, wind, ground cover, and terrain will affect the dog's scenting. Because you can't explain things to your dog, you can teach him to handle different conditions only by exposing him to them, but it does help in early training if you know what is probably happening to the scent so you can put your dog where he is apt to recover it before he gets frustrated. Chapter IV explains some environmental factors; you should personally verify scent behavior in each circumstance so that you recognize it quickly when it occurs during a real search.

Always do your best to understand what scent is like to your dog. Research has indicated the dog has at least a million and perhaps several trillion times our ability to detect an odor. What is only now being recognized is that there is a qualitative as well as a quantitative difference. With scent, dogs get a unique total configuration where we get only "an odor" (just as with sight we recognize "Johnny, hurt and exhausted," not merely "pink skin color" or some light rays with wavelengths from 580 to 680 nm).

The human brain turns an assortment of electromagnetic vibrations into a picture that it recognizes despite the addition of makeup, hats, and veils; despite the image's being reflected in a mirror, reproduced in a photograph, or even printed as black dots on gray newsprint. Note that the picture survives translation into entirely different electromagnetic vibrations from those we "saw" originally, and we would need a spectrum analyzer to identify components of either set.

So our dogs' brains process the nerve impulses stimulated by the assorted molecules reaching their nasal passages into "scent-pictures" that are recognizable despite the masking of perfumes, soap, campfire smoke, etc. Thus, you can understand why a dog need not "take scent" every few minutes on a search and may become impatient--as you would if given a mug-shot to study every time you turned around.

The big difference between a dog's "scent-picture" and a human's "sight-picture" is that the scent-picture leaves a trace wherever it has been that fades slowly or fluctuates, whereas the sight-picture requires a medium such as photographic paper or memory storage and is permanent so long as its medium remains intact. The information content of an aged scent trail may be likened to that of a series of water-streaked, sun-faded photographs, some of which are missing, seen in very dim light.

Extensive tests run by Neuhaus[*] established thresholds of perception and of recognition for aliphatic acids (present in sweat). As do humans, dogs **perceive** quantities of scent below those required to **recognize** the substance, and both thresholds may be lowered or raised by the presence of other substances which may or may not be detectable. As do humans, dogs experience nose fatigue when exposed to high scent concentrations (although they do not appear to screen disagreeable scents out mentally after a time), and they can pull a desired scent out of a background of stronger scents. The only difference is that dogs are much better at it.

The handler should be aware that volatiles like gasoline can saturate the nasal passages and temporarily impair scenting ability. However, the dog can learn to discriminate against such odors--it is on record that a police bloodhound successfully tracked a suspect through a machine shop full of motor oil and similar vapors. Some medicines (atropine, antispasmodics, anesthetics, antihistamines, and belladonna) depress scenting ability; caffeine and amphetamines temporarily stimulate it. We learn from this to

---

[*] W. Neuhaus, Die Riechschwellen des Hundes fur Jonon und Athylmercaptan und ihr Verhaltnis zu anderen Riechschwellen bei Hund und Mensch, *Z. Naturforsch*, **8**, 560-7, (1954).

take dogs out of the vehicle and walk them about in fresh air for awhile before putting them to a scent test, perhaps even giving them some water. We recognize that our dogs are not in condition to do scent work if on allergy treatment. We may allow them a sip from our coffee cup at lunch break on a long search ("uppers" are not recommended for either dog or handler!)

But when the actual search begins, the operating partner takes over. The manager wisely allows him to work, follows at a respectful distance, observes every indication and does his best to understand it, documents the results--but never, NEVER tries to take over the search function. He does not guide the dog, second-guess the dog on the basis of footprints in the sand or other non-scent clues, or force the dog on in a direction he finds unpromising. Even in training, the dog must be maneuvered (rather than guided or clued) into working where he will inevitably make a find. He must be convinced that his handler does not know where the subject of the search is to be found, that it is all up to him, and that he is entitled to be proud when he succeeds. Then, he will adopt your search objectives as his own and will pursue the scent with a devotion you will find hard to match. If you have really convinced him you don't know the subject's location, he will be frantically eager to take you there after he makes the find--especially if he is accustomed to receiving a treat when he brings you to the subject.

Even more difficult than concealing your prior knowledge in the training phase will be convincing your dog of your own genuine limitations. Puppies, very submissive dogs, and those with extensive obedience training are prone to believe that "Master knows everything." They think you can hear, scent, taste, feel textures, detect motion, and see in the dark as well as they do. It's hard to convey the fact that only in sighting distant still shapes and unusual colors by daylight, in using instruments to enhance your senses, and in correlating non-sensory data are humans superior.

Fortunately, eons of pack life have made it natural for the dog to indicate what his senses detect. When you see pricked ears, a rigid stance, a wagging tail suddenly stilled, you should ask "What is it?" even if you know or can guess. The longer you delay acknowledging what the dog wants to show you (provided you keep encouraging him to communicate), the more insistent he will become, the more obvious will be his signal, and the better he will learn how much you need him.

When you do acknowledge his signal, give immediate praise. As it becomes habitual for your dog to communicate to you everything he detects and to believe you won't know these things unless he tells you, be careful not to spoil it all by reprimanding him for doing so around the house. My breed, the Weimaraner, is particularly trying: mine tell me when the water bucket is empty, when a strange car or truck passes our gate, when the puppies should be put out, even when I should go to sleep and wake up. One Weimaraner insisted on telling his owner when his visiting nephew was about to load his pants, and when ignored, he would nip the toddler and try to drive him out into the yard as if to say, "That little whelp should have been housebroken long since!"

The other side of the dog's insistence on your acknowledging everything he scents or detects is the dog's response to what you feel. This generally appears shortly after the insistence, and it can be as rewarding as the insistence is irksome. All at once your dog knows what you want or need without your asking. You don't have to say, "No bark" or "Heel". This is especially welcome when you are ill or hurt; your erstwhile boisterous companion becomes quiet, gentle, caring. He even recognizes when you begin to feel overprotected and lies down a little way off, far enough not to bother you but close enough to know it should you need something he can fetch. All at once the partnership seems to jell; you and your dog become like two parts of one mind.

This is not, of course, a perpetual state. You still have times when your dog insists and you know better, when he takes it upon himself unnecessarily to "protect" you, or when one of you fails to recognize the other's legitimate concern. But in working together, if you do enough of it, your differences will vanish. You will be one in purpose, in persistence, and in sensitivity to every clue. You will no longer be reading your dog, nor he obeying you; your shared senses will together be trained on one objective: the search.

III. GETTING OFF ON THE RIGHT FOOT

Scent work has generally been classified into three different types--by humans, that is. Dogs do not recognize the distinction without being taught. The three are defined as follows:

TRACKING - nosing each and every footstep and working step by step along the ground; generally, the dog keeps his lead taut. The dog is always in harness and usually on a 20-to-40-foot lead. (American Kennel Club tracking, Schutzhund).

TRAILING - following a ground track but not step by step; typically, the dog's nose will go down for a sniff every 3 or 4 steps, and the dog may work several feet downwind of where the tracklayer actually walked. May be done on or off lead. (Police Bloodhound training, rescue dog on a long search. Bloodhounds are usually worked on lead because they become so engrossed with the trail that they must be restrained for their own safety.)

AIR SCENTING - testing the air flow for body scent rather than for ground scent; the dog works with head held high, except when sifting through debris, hunting avalanche victims buried in snow, etc. Usually done off lead. (Most German Shepherd search dog training, pointing and retrieving dog training.)

We humans may have made an artificial distinction, at least in the case of the first two. Look at it this way--the scent particles must be carried to the receptors inside the dog's nose by the air he inhales before he can detect them. Why, then, should the dog be taught to ignore the particles one inch above ground, or ten inches above ground, or re-exuded from nearby vegetation, or descending from on high? Left to himself, the dog will use all the traces present. Experience teaches him which type will lead him soonest to his goal under various conditions.

The "tracking dog" is most useful where the missing person's starting point is accurately known (the driver's seat of a parked car, the gate of a residence, etc.), where the track is relatively coherent, and where the search time is not excessive. In evidence search, "tracking" is most apt to turn up all the articles the person has dropped or hidden--unless, of course, he threw them away from him.

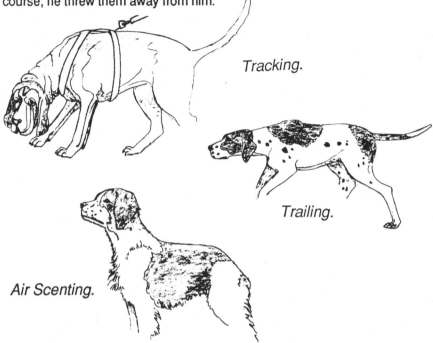

Tracking.

Trailing.

Air Scenting.

The "trailing dog" can sweep an area and find the start of a track where its exact location is unknown, can pick up an intermittent track repeatedly, and may even be able to "drop-track"; that is, follow a person to where he boards a vehicle and, when driven along the route taken, indicate where the person gets out and starts off on foot again. Some believe "trailing" is less fatiguing for the dog because sniffing track by track requires breath the dog could otherwise use for locomotion; thus a "trailing" dog can work longer before having to rest his muscles--and his nose, since intermittent scenting does not lead to sensory saturation as rapidly as does continuous scenting. You will probably see confirmation of this for yourself when you begin working tracks over a mile in length. Assuredly, the "trailing dog" covers more ground faster than the "tracking dog," shortcuts the loop where a track doubles back upon itself, and may go directly to a lost person who is walking in circles. In evidence search, he is more apt to find the gun thrown thirty feet into the bushes, or the loot dropped in the creek bed, than is the "tracking dog."

The "air scenting dog" is the best choice for finding avalanche or smoke victims before they suffocate. Turned loose at the edge of a picnic area, he may go directly to a lost child, saving hours of exposure that might be fatal. He may help locate a victim a thousand feet down a cliff or stranded at the same altitude on a ridge miles away that the dog taught rigorously to ignore air scent might never find. He is superior at locating multiple bodies in flood or earthquake debris, for he is trained to give a definite signal, called an "alert," when he comes upon **any** human scent. This very fact, however, limits his utility in an area full of grid searchers and casual hikers.

All forms of scenting have their place, and left to himself, the dog will do all three. It may seem strange, then, that most instructors single out a particular scent skill to teach first. Why not teach all of them together?

The main reason is human, not canine, limitation. We must know what the dog is doing in order to shape his ability to our needs, and while we our-selves are learning, we cannot easily observe three things at once. Second, if we apply to work with an SAR team, we must expect to be examined in each skill separately. If we want to pass the test for an AKC degree, we must get the dog to do "pure tracking".

Where, then, to start? Most people find tracking the easiest. Because the dog wears a harness and is worked on lead, there can be no question of his dashing off on some game of his own invention. There-fore, you can practice anywhere safely and persuade the dog to play **your** game. The tension in the lead, and the dog's posture seen at very short range, are two easy ways of "reading" your dog (much harder to learn when he is crashing through the brush fifty yards away). The attention you are forced to give to the track helps you learn how scent flow deviates from visible marks on the earth and changes its pattern with various conditions..

Both dog and handler will tend to drift into trailing naturally as their experience and the length and difficulty of the practice searches increase. For that reason, our lesson plan in this book lumps tracking and trailing together. If you want a "pure tracking dog," keep the tracks short and go on to AKC Tracking after you finish Lesson 4 of Tracking and Trailing. If you want to emphasize trailing, have extended tracks laid with many long legs. You can get the dog to do one or the other on command by using different words: "Work Close" and "Track It," for instance.

If your only interest is in air scenting, you can simply start with the Air Scent lesson plan. That way, however, your dog will not learn to discri-minate between one person's scent and another without considerable extra work, and you will not learn to read your dog as readily because you will not know what there is to read as well as when running a marked track. Furthermore, it is much easier to go from a strict, exacting discipline to loose control than to tighten up a relatively free style of working. Even dogs that have learned to air scent after becoming competent trackers must be given copious reminders when they return to tracking.

On the positive side, tracking lays a strong foundation for all the other scent skills. A tracking dog has learned to look for both people and articles, so he is easily taught to concentrate on one or the other (as in evidence search); to look for them in or near wrecks and collapsed buildings (as in disaster search); or to find them under water. The air scent dog who has first learned tracking will almost automatically distinguish between the trace of a lost person and that of another member of your rescue team--after all, he has been learning to disregard irrelevant crosstracks since the start of his training.

Record your progress. Whatever you choose to work on, be sure to keep a log. If you eventually take up Search & Rescue, the log provides evidence that you have appropriate preparation for searching. You may need it to apply for certification, or to protect yourself against lawsuits. If you are training for your own and your dog's benefit, the log reminds you of what you have done, how it worked out, and what needs additional practice. A handy form is shown below. The sheet is laid out to document a month's work, with each line representing a day's session. Attach to the back of the log sheet a sketch or map for each problem showing where the thing or person you searched for was hidden and where the dog actually went. This gives you a complete, permanent record of your progress in as much detail as needed to guide your training, with a convenient monthly summary to turn in to agencies you may work for.

TRAINING LOG

Dog __Jack__   Handler __Carol__   Month/Year __12 /89__

Date	Track/ Trail	Air Scent	Evi- dence	Agi- lity	Dis- aster	Map/ Compass	First Aid	Loca- tion	Description	Results
1	2 hr							Ski area	Intermediate track	Good finds. One loss, well recovered.

Illustration of monthly log sheet.

MAP OF PROBLEM

(Attach all maps for month to back of log for a complete record.)

Date _12 / 1_   Time laid _10:45 AM_ Time run _5:15 PM_ Wind Velocity _8-10_ mph

Temperature _52°_   Ground cover _Rock, pine needles_ Remarks _Light rain_

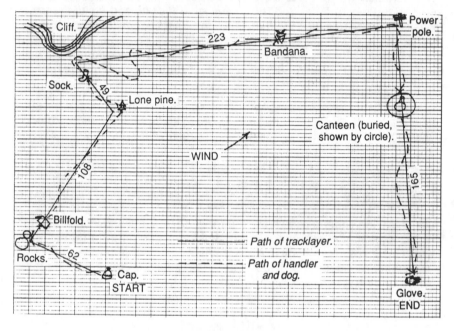

Sample map of a trail problem.

Pre-training. Some preliminary exercises will make scent work come easier, especially if your dog is very young.

1. <u>Acceptance of the lead</u>. Attach the lead to the dog's collar and let him drag it around while playing in the yard. When he stops paying attention to it, take up the end and hold it while the dog plays around you. At first, go with him when he dashes off. Then restrain him gently from going so fast. Finally, bring him to a stop by gradually increasing the pressure; hold him still at your side for a moment before letting him range again--show him the restraint is not forever.

2. <u>Controlled walking.</u> When the dog has accepted the lead, tell him cheerily, "Let's go for a walk." Start off briskly, encouraging the dog to go with you. Don't drag him, but give a little snap on the lead in the direction you want him to go if he persists in trying to run off on his own. Start this in a

large space where there is room for you to go with the dog at first, then encourage him to go with you by slapping your leg, holding out a treat, etc. Later put on his lead in a hall or other closed space where he is constrained either to go forward beside you or stay where he is. A snap to get him started is the last resort; say, "Let's walk" and step off briskly, and probably he will bound along. Again, DO NOT DRAG THE DOG.

3. "Go to" is a game you can play in the livingroom. A family member the dog especially likes should play with you. Hold the dog by the collar, face him toward your son, and say "Go to Johnny." Give him a little push in Johnny's direction. You can even go with him, if needed, to give him the idea. Johnny should greet him with open arms and praise or treat him. (Holding out a treat is one way to get the dog to come so you can praise him; give him the treat instantly when he arrives.) Then Johnny should hold his collar, point him in your direction, and say "Go to Mom/Dad." Again, praise or treat the dog on arrival. It's handy to be able to send your dog to a particular family member even if you don't want to do scent work. Advanced practice includes sending the dog to a friend--but be sure you teach the dog the friend's name before you try. If he hears the name without knowing he may have to use it, it can pass right over him.

4. Hide and seek grows naturally out of "Go to." Ask a family member to step around a corner out of sight and then say, "Go to Johnny." After praise, repeat, but this time have Johnny really hide and say, "Find Johnny." Expand this to hiding under a blanket that the dog must pull back or outside a door against which he must scratch for you to open in order to complete his find. CAUTION: have the dog find various people so that he doesn't decide he should search only for one.

5. Informal retrieve. For a young dog, start with an object that won't hurt new teeth, such as a sock with a knot in it. Most dogs like to pick up something their owner has worn. Wave the object under the dog's nose, encourage him to try to grab it, then throw it out 3 or 4 feet and release the collar with a little push toward the object while saying "Fetch!"

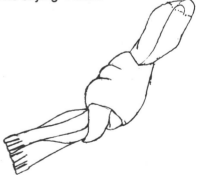

This works best if the dog reaches the object while it is still moving (prey-catching instinct). If the puppy doesn't pick it up, go to him and put it gently in his mouth; hold it there with one hand while you lead him with the other back to where you started. Praise or treat and take the object. If the puppy refuses to give it up, push it farther into his mouth (which forces his jaws open), snatch it out quickly, and throw it again at once.

He will probably run to capture it. You want the puppy to learn that the quicker he surrenders it, the sooner he gets to chase it again. Repeat at most five or six times in any one session; stop while the dog is still eager to retrieve. Next session use a different object; the dog should not get the idea he will retrieve only one thing. Later, hold the dog till the object stops moving, or even put him on a "stay" while you place the object some distance off. Do not hurry this part; go back to letting him chase the moving object if his eagerness wanes.

6. "Leave it." Don't use one of the dog's retrieving objects. When the puppy starts to pick up something you don't want him to have, say sharply "Leave it!" Run to him, take the object from his mouth, and put it back where it was. You may need to start with "No! Leave it!"

Practice until the dog will stop in the act of picking something up when he hears your command. A dog that will "leave it" readily is easier to have around the house. He can be called off from approaching a rattlesnake or your pet bird, and is prepared for the time when you want to stop him from picking up something other than the proper scent article or from jumping on a stranger. It is worthwhile to teach the dog to "leave it" on a hand signal as well as a verbal command.

6. "Find your toy." When the dog retrieves readily, throw the object around a corner, hide it under a towel, etc. The dog that will readily pick up objects--and "leave it" on command--goes easily into the recognition of scent articles in tracking or obedience. You now have the tools to direct him and to tell him when he has erred.

Basic principle. You must keep in mind that most dogs learn to do what you indicate, by praise or reward, you want them to do. Therefore, avoid accidentally training the dog to do something you will later want to forbid. It wastes your time, and it confuses or annoys the dog. Why this caution? Because a dog can form a habit from one or two occurrences that is almost impossible to break. Should your first tracks all be straight lines, your dog will assume every track is a straight line unless you spend several practice sessions teaching him otherwise. Should your tracklayer invariably drop objects to mark corners, your dog will assume that the track must turn every time he finds an object. Dogs have even more tendency than humans to jump to conclusions.

Furthermore, if you punish the dog for doing something that you praised previously, he will begin to question your judgment. You will lose his respect, and no amount of "correction" will regain it. He may obey, but not with good will. He may even become a dishonest dog, doing what he thinks you want rather than truly searching. It cannot be overemphasized:

TEACH ONLY WHAT YOU INTEND TO TEACH.

IV. WHERE DID THAT SCENT GO?

We are not going to guide our dogs, right? Nevertheless, we want to put our dogs where scent is apt to be found, encourage them in the best strategy to recover a lost track, recognize what performance we can reasonably expect, and avoid pulling them off a valid scent path. To do this, we need to know something about how scent behaves.

We need not debate what "scent" is: shed particles, gases produced by bacteria eating the particles, exhaled water vapor, sweat, or just molecules. We need only know that something is given off which gets to the nostrils and activates nerve impulses the brain interprets as scent. A good summary of the process is available (Pearsall-Verbruggen, Chapters 1-3), but for teaching purposes we need only recognize there is a substance that sticks to nearby objects after the thing it characterizes is gone and that can be detected over a considerable time.

Age Effects. Many have tried to measure how scent declines with age. This is difficult because seldom do other factors (e.g., temperature, humidity, air flow) stay constant. But suppose a stationary front wraps our area in heavy mist so that no wind blows, no heat is lost or gained, and the humidity stays close to 100% for a whole day. Experimenters A and B lay a number of tracks precisely equal in difficulty and run them with dogs that are equal in ability (not easy to obtain). Judging the amount of scent that remains from the ease with which the dog works, they plot points as shown at left.

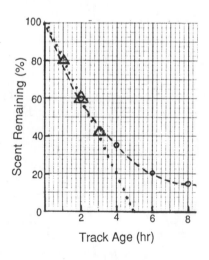

A runs three dogs over tracks aged 1, 2, and 3 hours. His estimates of 80%, 60%, and a bit over 40% (small triangles) lead him to conclude that scent falls off at 20% per hour (as shown by dotted line), so his dogs will find no scent at 5 hours or after.

B runs four dogs over tracks aged 2, 4, 6, and 8 hours. He also sees 60% on the 2-hour-old track,but after that his estimates are 35%, 20%, and 15% (small circles). From the shape of the curve that these points define (dashed line), he concludes, "The decline is not linear; it is exponential. The scent will never reach zero, although it will come close. At the rate it is going, there will still be 0.005% left at 40 hours; and since dogs can detect a few parts per trillion, they can still track it." A claims that B exaggerated his dogs' performance but cannot deny that B's dog was still following **something** at 8 hrs.

Note how A and B's interpretations are affected by their prior convictions. A does not believe a dog can run a really old track; therefore, he would not even try one of his on a track older than 3 hrs, and at that early point the difference between a linear and an exponential decline is just beginning to be detectable--he can dismiss it as a lapse in his power to estimate. Although B has no more experience than A with aged tracks, he has heard of dogs finding objects and people that have been missing for days, not hours, and he is unwilling to dismiss these claims without a test; his results indicate to him that his own dogs are capable of the kind of performance he has heard described.

Many observations, by many people, tend to support B. Even some who say the scent is zero after such-and-such a length of time draw a curve with an exponential shape to describe the decline. Why does it matter? Because if B is correct, no matter how old the track, **some** scent remains to be found. We are not asking the dog to do the impossible.

Humidity and Temperature. Scent does not decline monotonically. Sometimes it increases. A track that seems faint after hours of sun and wind may resurge under a light rain or morning dew. Remember that dry air picks up fewer scent particles and tends to seal the surfaces of ground features so that particles they have absorbed cannot escape. Moisture may free these trapped particles. A heavy downpour, however, washes particles back into the ground or away with the runoff, largely wiping out the track.

Temperature interacts with humidity. Heat increases the activity of molecules so that more can leave solid objects, and water vapor carries scent with it as it evaporates. When exposed surfaces dry out, evaporation declines and less scent becomes detectable. Temperature acts independently as well. The rate of molecular heat exchange between the air and the earth depends on the temperature difference between them; the heat flow carries scent with it. The net radiant energy flow into or out of the earth is also a scent carrier; when more is received from the sun and/or reflected by the atmosphere than the earth emits, scent diffusion declines. This earth outflow is what causes scent from buried objects to rise through a snowpack and become detectable; ice layers in the snow and energy reflected back from clouds may hinder or block the diffusion.

The implications of all this are, luckily, less complex. Early morning is an ideal time to search, evening and night are good; midday is not. If you must search an area on a hot afternoon, you should report a low probability of detection so that the area will be searched again under better conditions if no one is found promptly. On a sunny day, shaded and north-facing slopes are apt to be more productive than south-facing slopes. Although a light rain is generally helpful, a heavy one will wash scent off of exposed surfaces and may carry it down into the ground. In a downpour, look for patches of scent in sheltered places (in caves, beneath ledges, under heavy brush--also look for footprints!). Evaporation from moist wood (logs beside path, boardwalks, picnic tables) may carry the scent you seek. Heat sources (fire, hot springs) will diffuse scent; heat sinks (cool flows of water) will draw it away--but you may find strong traces on the edge of them.

Air Flow, Wind, Terrain. Patterns of air flow result from temperature and air pressure differences. It is a good habit to follow the TV weather-casts, especially those with satellite maps, if you often engage in searching. You may not be able to wait for the next one when you get a call-out. This overview, plus daily observation of weather patterns in your own locality, will help you understand what you see in the field.

Scent rises in a cone from each source (article, footprint, person). On level ground when the air is still, the cone rises straight up, its diameter approximating its height above the surface. This gives rise to good scenting. The diagrams on p. 25 show how the cones act in various situa-tions; the most productive search areas are crosshatched.

In rapidly rising air currents, cones may be very tall and thin--the dog's nose may have to be directly above the source to detect the scent. After sunset when the valley floors are cooling but the peaks are still in sunlight, we see what is called "lofting": air stable at ground level but rising rapidly above. Because air flow tends to follow earth contours, some scent may be found along the ridges and upper slopes.

At daybreak and for a short time after, we get the opposite condition, "fumigating." The rising sun warms the ground and the air immediately above it rapidly; the scent cones are cooler than this air and diffuse downward, spreading out along level ground or downslope in the mountains. The message for the dog handler is, "Get in the field early and take advantage of it."

Scent cones in still air.

Lofting.

Fumigating.

Inversion.

Looping.

Gusty wind.

Rough terrain.

Scent pool with leakage.

A stable cold air layer aloft with warmer air beneath will cause an "inversion": smoke hangs low over the valleys, and you hear smog alerts on your car radio. In this situation, the scent cones become short and fat. They may congregate just below the cold air layer and spread out for miles. If your dog alerts on a narrow altitude span along a mountain slope but loses the scent above and below it, he may be detecting a person at that altitude on the next mountain, or two or three mountains over. Get on your radio and suggest to Rescue Base that the coordinator ask what other dog handlers are seeing at the same contour line. The directions of several alerts, plotted on a map, may point at or circle a single spot miles off that a helicopter could check out.

Rapid cooling aloft when the sunlit ground is warming the surface air may cause scent cones to rise until they cool, drop to earth, heat up and rise again over and over, a condition called "looping." Dogs may alert repeatedly but without direction, possibly straight up. Mapping where the alerts are seen may produce a line that leads to the victim.

In addition to these vertical air movements, often called "turbulence," we have the horizontal air movement we all know as "wind." A steady wind will change the scent-cone cross sections from circles to ovals and displace the cones in the downwind direction. This may cause even the close-tracking dog to work a bit downwind of the true course. The trailing dog will work tree-lines or ridges where the dispersing scent becomes trapped, and rain or snow carries it down to the ground.

A steady wind over open ground spreads scent conically away from a stationary person. An experienced air scent dog that runs back and forth, back and forth in an ever-narrowing pattern is working up a lateral cone toward a scent source at its apex.

How far upwind you should look for clues depends on wind strength: a stronger wind carries heavier particles farther. It also "scrubs" the scent off non-absorbing surfaces (rock, gravel). Estimate the wind velocity as you practice, and remember its effect on your dog's pattern to help you interpret his actions on a real search. Caution: test the wind at the dog's nose level, not up by your face. A strip of trail tape tied at your knee can serve as a wind gauge.

And then there's the gusty wind. It comes from now this way, now that; constantly changes velocity; and spreads the scent cones all over the map. The dog gets frustrated, you get upset. Only the close-tracking dog can work well in such weather. Fortunately, the gusts do not often persist for long and you'd best wait it out--preferably in shelter, for this condition often marks the leading edge of a storm front.

Terrain has local effects on wind and hence on scent movement. When the sun is low, mountain peaks and ridges get more heat than shadowed valleys. As the air above them rises, an upslope current forms to replace it. After dark, these exposed areas lose heat rapidly into space, cooling the air around them so that it becomes heavier than the air below and drains away downslope. Consequently, your tracking dog will tend to work above the actual trail in early morning and below it after sunset; you should work your air scent dog high on the ridges at sunrise and along the bottoms of the valleys as night thickens.

Where a trail crosses an arroyo or creek on a steep slope, your dog may alert both up and down, perhaps even taking a few steps to each side before continuing to track in the original direction. He is not misleading you, he is simply indicating that both upward and downward flows of the scent have occurred--telling you that the trail is at least a few hours old.

If an obstacle bars its way, the air flows around it and may form eddies on the lee side. Scent may precipitate there, but the direction it came from may be hard to determine. Air rising along a cliff face will tend to overshoot and return to earth some distance from the brink; scent carried up from the cliff's base is best detected back a hundred paces or so from the edge. Such obstacles as groves of trees will absorb scent from the wind, and the dog can detect it by working along them.

Pools. The most important effect of terrain which we must take into account is the scent pool. A hollow in rough ground, a clearing among the trees, even a courtyard or square between buildings will cause air scent to be trapped and pool in the open part.

This causes a noticeable difficulty for the search dog. If the dog is attempting to track, the pall of air scent hanging close to the ground may displace at nose-level the track scent he is trying to follow. The air scenter will find cause to alert, but unless the pool is small and the subject in the middle of it, he may have trouble detecting the exact location. When someone asks you to hide for an air scenter "long enough to create a good scent pool," he means long enough for your scent to fill the small hollow in which you hide and overflow so the dog needs only to get in the general neighborhood to detect you. He does not mean long enough for your scent to fog the entire valley bottom, as can happen when there is little or no air movement.

The dog's instinct, rightly, is to locate the perimeter of the scent pool and define its extent, then fine-search segments of it. A linear track overhung with a wide pall of scent elicits behavior called "quartering"--working back and forth from one edge to the other. This is intelligent of the dog, for the edges of the scent-stream give him a direction of travel whereas in the middle of the stream surrounded by an equal density of particles on all sides, he gets no indication of where he should be headed. How unfortunate it is that so many tracking judges believe quartering is reprehensible; this is the dog's best technique for maintaining forward progress in a pool.

Without quartering--

dog is confused.

Quartering--edge of

scent path gives

direction.

In still air on flat or cupped terrain, each scent article forms a pool that grows radially larger with time. Coming upon a discarded canteen, for example, your best hope of tracking the owner (if you can see no foot-prints) is to circle it with the dog, far enough out so you are beyond the edge of the pool, and notice where the dog's head goes down. Continue around the circle a second time; if the dog's head drops at the same place again and he leads off away from the object, go with him.

Sometimes you can't count on scent pools. A person, animal, or bird gives off much less scent when it lies still on the ground than when it moves briskly (think how often a bird dog will miss a hen pheasant huddled down in the grass). Moreover, the scent emitted is proportional to exposed body surface area. Therefore, when you are following a fairly strong trail and suddenly your dog seems to detect little or nothing, make a careful visual inspection of the nearby area. The person may well have stopped moving and huddled down in a plastic trash bag as the survival books recommend, in which case the scent pool around him will be extremely small even if he has been there quite some time.

I believe Rudi and I once missed a lost hunter this way in a mountain snowstorm. When the man crawled out of his shelter after the snow and climbed to the base-camp fire, he said he had burrowed into the branches of a downed tree that I recalled passing several times as we circled trying to recover the scent. We had examined the mound's edges but had not probed all the way to the stump. The man sleeping out the storm was not emitting much scent; and what there was, the falling snow carried back into the drift on the ground even as it hid the marks on the crust his elbows and knees had made crawling in. That time my own eyes and brain would have served better than Rudi's nose.

These, then, are factors we must understand if we are to help our dogs, not hinder them. Look for unusual circumstances as you practice, and you will know better what you're up against in real-life emergencies.

V. I NEED TO KNOW, TOO

No matter what kind of scent work you are doing, your dog must learn to inform you when he has made a find. If searching far out or in heavy cover, he must return close enough for you to catch his signal. On the American Kennel Club tests, you may be disqualified if you must noticeably restrain your dog to make him indicate an article he is walking over; he is expected to indicate it on his own. A very independent dog (the best kind for scent work) may get irked with you if you become self-conscious in the test situation and put too much pressure on the lead. Such dogs may put on a very convincing act ("What article? I don't smell any article") unless they are trained to give a specific find indication to the point where it becomes second nature.

In scent-training parlance, the dog's coming back to get you after he finds is known as a "recall," and his taking you to the article or person is referred to as a "refind." In the simplest case, the dog combines refind and recall: he snatches up the article and brings it to you. Some-times the recall is omitted: the dog sits, stands, or lies down at the find or advises you by voice: a "barking refind."

Teach the refind early. The dog learns it quickly while he still has a strong desire for you to reward him. If you wait, the dog may come to regard the find itself as his reward, and you will have lost a major tool for inducing refind signals. Therefore, begin teaching an appro-priate refind as soon as the dog has mastered the basics of one search technique.

Choose the type of refind according to the work you will most fre-quently do. A large dog barking near a small child or a shy person he has found may scare the victim. A dog scratching at a collapsed building may trigger another cave-in, whereas digging in avalanche snow may uncover the person's face and save his life. A dog picking up lost keys is being efficient, but with stolen goods he is destroying evidence (which should be left untouched for the investigators) and with cocaine he is risking his own life if even a small bit gets in his mouth. Some dogs choose a signal of their own. If you need to replace it with a signal of your choice, for safety or other reasons, the earlier you make the change, the easier it will be.

How do we get the dog to stop picking up the article and switch to another refind method? We couple the dog's desire for reward with frustration: we tie down the article or use one too heavy for the dog to move; we have the hidden person lie quiet, as if unconscious. Faced with such a problem, the dog is apt to yelp--for a barking alert, immediately run to him and say, "Good speak, good speak." (It doesn't hurt to teach him to "speak" on verbal command before you start.) Wait for the bark and then acknowledge his find several days in succession to fix the barking alert in his mind.

For a position signal, pretend not to hear the yelp but command, "Sit" or "Down" or whatever you desire, then run to the dog and praise him when he does as you wish. Wait longer and longer before giving the verbal command until the dog uses the desired behavior on his own; then omit the command altogether.

For a classic recall and refind, ignore the yelp and the dog's motions until he comes frantically back to you. He may jump on you, tug at your clothing, etc. When he does, praise him and say, "What is it? Show me!" and let him take you to the find--at first on lead, later without it.

You need not restrict your dog to a single refind signal. The ideal search dog gives different find indications for an article, a moving person, an inert human, a small clue such as a footprint in mud or snow. You can tell the dog what general type of refind you want by being consistent in the garb for each exercise (a harness for tracking, a vest for air scent, a special collar for disaster work, a transmitter for avalanche) and then responding only to the appropriate refind for that activity. It is much easier to read your dog on a genuine find if you have demanded a consistent type of refind in your practice sessions.

Finer differentiation of the refind more often involves training yourself than the dog, because the dog has a different bark or different manner of doing his refind act depending on what he has found and all you have to do is notice. Of course, if your avalanche dog digs out feet rather than faces, he should be shown that the quickest path to his reward is at the other end of the subject--here, behavior shaping is definitely in order.

The hardest part of teaching the recall/refind is getting the dog always to complete the whole process. Some dogs will run off as soon as they have attracted your attention. If your dog does this, turn back the way you were walking before he came to you and stroll along as if you didn't get the message. Most dogs will come running to you again, even more insistent. This time, give the dog no opportunity to run off--snap the lead on his collar and let him take you to the find under restraint. When he does so without hesitation at your "Show me" command (a week or two weeks into refind training), use the lead only every other or every third time, finally not at all.

A few dogs get the idea that the job is done when they have found something to their own satisfaction. As a puppy, my dog Simon saw no need to tell me about it: "After all, she knows everything!" He would buzz the article or the person's hidingplace, then race off in search of something new. The day he found two joggers and a man walking a Cocker Spaniel before deigning to come back and lead me to the woman and child he located first, I knew I had to take action. Some hard thinking as well as intensive practice finally cured this fault.

Aside from realizing I did not know unless he told me, Simon had to learn two things: a find was not complete until he united me with the subject, and he must finish one find before dashing off to make another. Fortunately, his intense joy at finding was strong enough that I needn't fear weakening his motivation. I excused him from regular classes for a month and took him far out into the backcountry, where there was nothing to find except my husband or an object he planted. I kept Simon on lead for both air scent and tracking. That way I could see his alert because he was always within sight and could use the lead to bring him back for the "Show me" command. When he dependably came to me on his own after establishing the location, I started putting more objects out to be found, and finally we returned to working off lead.

Many air scent handlers use a "bringsel"--a rolled piece of leather or other object attached by a short cord to the dog's collar, which the dog reaches down and seizes in his teeth at the find. (Various bringsel designs and their application are described in the Air Scent Lesson Plan.) When the dog comes back holding the bringsel in his mouth, the handler is sure a find has been made. I thought training Simon to use a bringsel would improve his refind.

First, Don carried the bringsel with him when he hid and gave it to the dog when he found him, saying, "Take it to Lue." Then we hung the bringsel on the collar and Don put it in Simon's mouth when he sent him back to me. Finally he urged him to reach down for it himself. Simon loved that. Once, when the bringsel tore loose in underbrush, he dashed back and seized Don's cap so he would have something to bring to me. But Simon's pellmell pace resulted in a lot of lost bringsels. Further, he liked to carry it so much that he would reach down and grab it when he first caught scent, before he had actually pinned down the location, causing many premature recalls and refinds. We therefore abandoned the bringsel. I taught Simon to recall only after he made sure he had something to show me, which has worked much better.

Some dogs give a recall indication that is too subtle to catch your attention. This is easily corrected. Just pretend, if you have a doubt, that you saw nothing at all (including the dog). The dog will then make a stronger effort. Praise and respond to the indication you prefer. It may take some doing to ignore a dog that is jumping on you, but if you make clear that you don't recognize this wild thing as your good dog until he gives the signal you want, you will eventually prevail. When the dog's desire for reward has become secondary to his joy of accomplishment, frustration is the most powerful tool you have.

A word of warning: watch your dog carefully and don't let his frustration level rise above what he can tolerate. You don't want him to get turned off on searching! If he acts desperate, run to him instantly and praise him; allow him time to become more sure of himself, then try it again. When his self-confidence is high enough, the dog will not permit you to ignore his refind indication, any more than he will let you pull him off a "hot" track. If one sign doesn't work, he will try another. Close observation of the dog's behavior and good timing of your reaction will make any dog not only willing to communicate but insistent on it.

VI. WE CAN'T LOSE IF WE KEEP TRYING

At first the whole thing was a game, in which the humans laid out a puzzle for the clever dog to unravel. Or perhaps it was a stunt, with treats and praise for outstanding performance. But one day the dog goes on a scent path with an intensity that has no play about it. The humans are shrugged aside, the treats ignored. The praise is accepted impatiently. Called in for rest and a drink of water, the dog is back on his feet before the handler is ready, sniffing at the bag that contains the scent article or pulling hard to get on up the trail. It doesn't matter that there may be exercises in the book you haven't even tried, or that the extra reading never got done. Suddenly, all at once, your dog is "search ready."

It didn't just happen. Amazing as it may seem at the moment, this readiness is the natural outcome of certain things you have been doing since the start. If it does not appear as soon as you wish or if a thoroughly miserable experience seems to have soured your dog, you may want to redouble your efforts in motivational techniques.

1. Every search has a pay-off. In early training, you will see to it that your dog finds the last object on each track, even if he misses some in between. As you progress to unmarked tracks for which you only refer to the map after the running, carry the initial scent object with you so that, should you become hopelessly lost and further attempts at recovery seem pointless, you can throw the object out ahead of your dog, let him find it, and reward him as if it had been the original.

Likewise, the air scent dog should never be put on a "dry" area. Some large dog-training groups do not realize this and will send out six or eight teams to assigned areas of which only two or three contain a victim. If you find yourself in that predicament, the best you can probably do is radio the team in the area adjoining yours and arrange for your dog to find them and their dog to find you. Better yet, make sure every practice area will contain at least one victim before you sign up to participate--and no, don't assume because they are more experienced than you that whatever they do is wise. It is of course true that you can demonstrate how your dog searches without making a find, but what you are trying to instill is your dog's conviction that he cannot and will not quit until he does make a find. Your dog's progress should take precedence over any group's testing practices.

No matter what kind of scent exercise you are doing, stick to this principle: quit only on a success. This even applies on a real search when you are recalled to base camp because a find has been made by another team or conditions are becoming too hazardous for searchers to remain in the field. If you cannot arrange to "find" another team while you both are returning to base, you can at least arrange to stop with another team outside the hazard zone and each hide for the other there. Naturally, you will give your dog a "Wait" command while you debrief and transport to the new area, saving the "Search over" signal for the moment after the arranged find.

2. Every find is an achievement. The dog's motivation is in large measure a reflection of the handler's attitude. If you are not a demonstrative person, you may have to learn to express yourself in more obvious ways than are natural to you. A proud, quiet smile is not going to tell your dog how great you think he is. It will take an energy-charged voice, hugs, pats, maybe even kisses or a full-scale wrestling match.

Don't think of this as pretending or "putting on." Think of it, rather, as communicating--positive feedback, if you will. You honestly and truly are delighted when your dog does well; the dishonest thing is to hide it. "Yes, you were wonderful but it isn't proper for me to show it" is the kind of muddy human thinking that frustrates and bewilders a dog. If you feel he was wonderful, let it out. Don't be self-conscious or worry about other people laughing at you. Other people don't matter; the important relation here is between you and your dog. You have to tailor your expression to what your dog understands and desires.

There should, of course, be degrees of praise. An intermediate article or the first alert on an elusive scent doesn't rate the same recognition as digging out a buried jewel cache or leading the handler to an injured victim. In fact, disproportionate praise in the middle of a search may distract the dog from the work that remains to be done. By observing your dog's reactions, you should soon know how to signal your approval in a supporting, not an interfering, manner. The sequence is: dog acts, you react, dog reacts to your reaction, you react to dog's reaction. An impartial third party can often watch your handling and help you communicate more effectively with your dog.

You must never forget to acknowledge your dog's work. When an injured victim is found, the handler often gets so wrapped up in radioing back to base and treating the victim that the dog, who made it all possible, is overlooked. Praise your dog first--it only takes a fraction of a second to let him know you appreciate what he's done. The full reward may wait until the victim is stabilized and the supporting evacuation team is on its way, but the basic acknowledgment should be immediate.

3. Demonstrate your reliance on your dog. Give him freedom to use his senses as he sees fit, so long as he keeps working. During practice, you must sometimes tell the dog what technique will best succeed that day, under those conditions, so he will know what to adopt in the future. For instance, when you induce him to keep his nose close to the ground scent in gusty wind, he gets positive directional clues instead of the scattered traces found higher up. With experience, he will know better than you what approach is most productive, and you must let him make the decision.

Trust the signals he gives you. Be especially alert for the dog's body language that says, "You didn't get what I was telling you; come on, try again." If the dog wants you to look at something, do so. Not only will you strengthen mutual communications, you may learn of an ability in the dog that you never suspected.

Rudi taught me that he could stand beside a path and screen a passing file of strangers for the one he was seeking. Simon taught me that he could indicate which of many visible tracks in the snow was the one made by his subject; I radioed its appearance to a ski team who cut the trail higher on the mountain and found the missing woman before we--or hypothermia-- could get to her.

Follow up every direction sign your dog gives, either personally or by advising Rescue Base or another team if it leads beyond your assigned area. In the latter case, do your best to let your dog know you have acted on the information. You can try, "Good boy, John will check it out; now let's finish combing this region," or even getting John to say, "Good boy" on the radio. Don't ignore a sign from your dog, no matter how farfetched it may seem. Probably no handler can say with complete honesty that he has NEVER broken this rule, but it's always a mistake.

4. Keep your expectations reasonable. You cannot demand a find; you can only ask for your dog's best effort. The subject may be in a completely different area, so that even locating a clue is impossible. The scent may be draining down into the ground cover rather than rising into the air where it can be detected. Make allowance for possible scent hazards realized all too clearly by the dog but perhaps not obvious to you. Be patient with your partner; you don't know how often he has patiently accepted your refusal to see what from his viewpoint was obvious.

Do what you can to mitigate bad conditions--cold, snow and ice, heat, lack of shade. Shorthaired dogs should have coats that protect their undersides when searching in deep snow covered by an ice crust and should be expected to swim in cold water only short distances, followed by a speedy warm-up. Dark- colored dogs should not be kept out in full sun on hot days, even those that may not seem so hot to you (remember, most of your body is elevated above the ground cover where there's a breeze to cool it). All dogs should be watered frequently, both to rehydrate their tissues and to moisten the nasal passages that make scenting possible. All dogs deserve a trail snack at least as often as their handlers, for they may cover five times as much ground as a human and expend many times as much energy per hour. A dog that is suffering physically cannot maintain his concentration--think of the last time you tried to complete a difficult task with a blinding headache.

<u>5. The dog should enjoy searching.</u> We refer here not to frivolous enjoyment or fun, but to total engrossment in the task, the good feeling of using every ability you have, the comfortable oneness with your partner, the satisfaction of doing something that really matters. Your dog feels pride of accomplishment when you do, so try to achieve this in every practice--a higher level in long field sessions, and the highest level of all in a real search.

Boredom, haste to get this over with and do something else, exhaustion past the point of caring, frustration with your seeming lack of progress-- all these destroy enjoyment. If your own condition prevents your working with a positive attitude, it is better not to work that day at all. The search should be a strong, clean, exhilarating experience even when you're both tottering with fatigue. Keep hold of that though your instructions are ambiguous, the logistics are poor, the weather is frightful, the support team is of negative assistance. Keep your purpose clearly in mind so that your own persistence will not flag, and it will echo back to you from your dog.

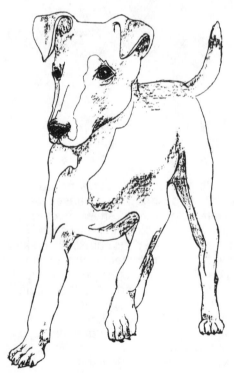

A search-ready dog.

VII. LESSON PLANS

The basic motivation for this book was to provide detailed, step-by-step outlines so that the inexperienced handler could train his own dog and the seasoned handler with a particularly difficult dog could pick up some new techniques. The lessons are also designed to serve as an orderly training guide for class work.

Both TRACKING AND TRAILING and AIR SCENT are intended to start a dog in scent work, but those who want an all-around scent dog will achieve their goal more easily if they begin with TRACKING AND TRAILING. If you want to undertake any project where the dog must understand how to work with restraint, the tracking approach is essential. After completing this outline, the dog is well prepared to branch out into EVIDENCE SEARCH or DISASTER SEARCH, whereas in AIR SCENT the dog has not learned the discipline and tolerance of restraint needed for the more exacting skills. The dog that has completed the first four or five lessons of TRACKING AND TRAILING can be polished for exhibitions and formal tests with the AKC TRACKING outline.

How often is it necessary to train? For steady progress, the dog and handler should work every other day, or three to four times a week. To maintain the skills already acquired takes two sessions a week. If the dog and handler can manage to work only once a week, they will probably slip back. Very few manage to keep their momentum over a seven-day gap, and the frustration accompanying failure at a task that may have gone well on first try will probably cause them to give up their training entirely after several weeks. Every month or so, a day-long field session in unfamiliar territory will help to maintain alertness and enthusiasm, as well as furnishing a good review.

How long should a dog stay on each exercise or step in training? Unfortunately, there is no one answer that applies to all dogs. The early lessons in each outline should be repeated three to six times or until essentially mastered (which will depend on the dog's quickness at picking up new skills and the regularity with which the handler is able to train). For the group training approach, each lesson is designed to be used for a week's class session and the intervening home work. If several members of the group find a lesson particularly difficult, it can be repeated a second or even a third week. The THINGS TO THINK ABOUT at the end of each lesson provide variations and extensions of the week's problem to absorb the attention of the class members who had no difficulty.

Dogs remember best their first success at any new activity. If the first way they try to complete a task works, that is the way they will try to do the task each time they encounter it in the future. If they are taught another approach that the handler prefers, they may accept it after many repetitions; but if months or years later they have difficulty applying it, they will tend to revert to their original technique.

That's why it is vital to make the first try a success. As handler, you must prepare thoroughly. Read over the instructions; make sure exactly what you are going to do. Then do the thing right, and see to it that the dog succeeds. Praise or reward him thoroughly. And stick to that basic, successful technique. You can build on it, elaborate it, but **don't** alter it. If you try method after method of doing the same thing, the dog will think that you don't know what you want or else that you are trying to trick him, and either way you lose his respect.

This does not mean you will repeat and repeat the same exercise--to do so courts boredom of both dog and handler. A bored dog may refuse to work at all, do it "his own way" which may include rounding up all the squirrels and rabbits in the country, or do it in a lackadaisical manner that suggests he really doesn't care whether he finds anyone. Bored people turn off their minds: they stop trying to read the dog, to observe the effects of wind and weather, or to understand the dog's problems. Both partners must remain alert, keeping their minds on the task and on each other.

Fortunately, every exercise in a real environment is subject to endless variation. Don't try to make today's problem just like yesterday's--you can't anyhow, and the surest preventive of boredom is to add or change something.

| NEVER DO ANYTHING TWICE IN EXACTLY THE SAME WAY. |

TRACKING AND TRAILING

LESSON PLAN

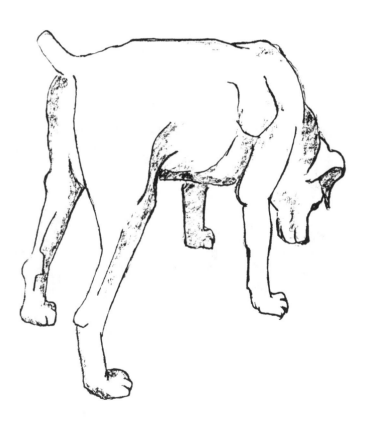

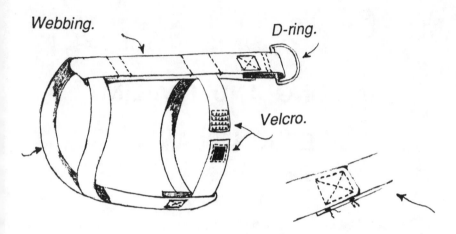

Webbing.

D-ring.

Velcro.

Detail of stitching (note that knots are between layers to prevent wear from friction).

Construction of non-restrictive tracking harness.

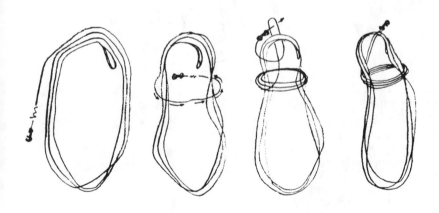

How to coil the tracking lead.

TRACKING AND TRAILING LESSON PLAN

Note: Because "trailing" may correctly be called "extended tracking" and both are taught the same way, we use the terms interchangeably. The dog doesn't see any difference between tracking and trailing until you teach him.

MATERIALS

The equipment for a tracking or trailing dog includes a non-restrictive harness, a 20-to-40-foot lead, and a variety of scent articles. Because the harness and lead furnish a clear signal that you want the dog to track, not to heel, they should be used from the very first exercise.

Harness and lead. A non-restrictive harness is one that does **not** have a band across the base of the neck that will hinder the dog's breathing if he lowers his nose to the ground. The "roading" or "sled dog" harness will not work. Non-restrictive harnesses can be purchased, but at Los Alamos we generally buy a 50-ft cotton web lead (nylon tears up your hands if your dog pulls hard and also may wear thin places in the dog's fur), then use 10 feet to make a harness according to the pattern at left.

The remaining 40 feet of lead has a snap sewn into one end and a marker at the 20-ft point--a strip of bright-colored cloth or yarn is best (loops sometimes catch on snags).

How to coil the lead. Starting from the handler end, wind the lead around your elbow and hand until about 3 feet remain. Take 3 or 4 turns around the coil, loop the rest through the top of the coil, and draw the snap through the loop as shown at left. Now attach the snap to the dog's collar and use the whole coil as a short lead to walk to the starting point; then pull the snap out of the loop, clip it to the harness, throw the coil back behind you, and it will uncoil smoothly by itself.

Scent articles. Use a variety of items; you don't want the dog to find only gloves. One litter of puppies I had got the idea from watching older dogs return with gloves that "tracking = glove finding." On walks in the National Forest they proudly collected archer's gloves, hunter's gloves, assorted work gloves, mittens, ski gloves, etc. So use bandanas, caps, shoes, T-shirts, billfolds, and sometimes gloves. At first, select medium-large, highly visible objects that hold plenty of scent: leather and cloth are better than plastic or metal. If you expect to use food as a reward, choose objects you can put treats inside. If you use a tug-of-war or play retrieve, the "tuggie" or toy can be the scent article at the trail's end.

Are you planning to lay the track yourself? Then use articles you have worn. Is someone else to lay the track? Then have him bring articles, or furnish new ones fresh from the store in plastic packages and let him open them. Note that laundering, sun, and wind do not remove all traces of scent; dogs will select their owner's freshly laundered clothes off a line in preference to others. After your dog has experience, he can disregard your scent on an article and discriminate for unfamiliar scent on it, but don't expect this at first. Let him concentrate on connecting the article scent with the foot trail scent (as these are not identical, the task is hard enough without two scents on the article).

HOW TO LAY A TRACK

The first tracks are difficult because you must know exactly where they lie so you can tell whether your dog is following them, yet your dog should not know where they lie except by scent. In addition, you must avoid teaching the dog that tracks follow a set pattern. If you start by running several straight lines to an article, you may waste a lot of time teaching the dog how to handle the first turn. Only when I watched naive baby pups blithely follow a rabbit track that turned every which way, even doubling back, did I realize the "first turn" problems came from having taught my dog that "tracks are straight lines".

The tracklayer should count steps while walking and record the total for each leg on a map. Counting can be done subconsciously when you get used to it. Steps can be converted to yards or meters, but then you just have to convert them back, so why not work with the number of paces.

Who should the tracklayer be? You can do it yourself, right up to where you need unmarked tracks to test how well you read your dog. It is best, though, to vary the tracklayer or the dog may assume "Track it" means to find a particular person. (Some dogs will track only individuals to whom they have been introduced.) Other dog trainers are best; they understand your problems. To use someone unfamiliar with tracking, stick numbered cards (1, 2, etc.) on bushes to mark out a trail. Have the person remove the cards in sequence, dropping articles at 1, 4, and 7 (for example) while turning left at the other odd numbers and right at the even ones. At first let a week or more elapse before you have the person remove the numbers and drop the articles, or else scent from when you laid the track will confuse the dog. This method is great for demonstrations.

To be sure the track makes a straight line (as for AKC tracking), choose two landmarks--one on the horizon, one in the near distance--and keep them lined up as you walk. Nearing the desired length of that track leg, choose a horizon landmark in the new direction and proceed slowly until a useful near-distant landmark comes into line with it. Note the angle of the turn on your map and the number of paces for that leg before going on.

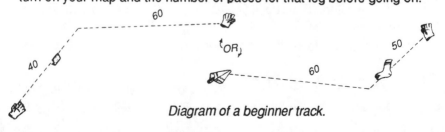

Diagram of a beginner track.

LESSON 1 - THE FIRST PRACTICE TRACK

The track should be laid according to the pattern on the facing page, preferably 24 hours in advance--in no case less than 4 hours. The cloud of air scent hovering along the tracklayer's path should have time to blow away so that the most obvious "foreign" scent present will be that of the actual ground track and articles. To avoid undesired scent pools, the tracklayer should walk the path and drop the articles without pause, but he can ignore wind direction. By the time the track is run, the wind will have changed.

Start. Put on the dog's harness. Scan the map, and remember it--you want your full attention on the dog while running the track. Take the dog, lead attached to his collar, to the first article and point at it; say, "Take scent". Unsnap the lead from the collar, snap it to the D-ring of the harness, and drop the remaining coils of lead out behind. Say, "Track it" to encourage the dog along the track. If the dog isn't interested, pick up the article, tease him with it, play tug-of-war, or otherwise make him want it. Then throw the article out a few feet ahead as you tell him to track it, and repeat until the dog is following the scent trail rather than the visual path (test by throwing the article behind a rock or clump of grass, out of sight but on the scent trail ahead; this trail will dominate the scent pool forming around the article in the short time before the dog makes his find).

First Leg. Stay right beside your dog, holding the lead with your left hand close to the D-ring. Continue to point at the track with your right hand and say,"Track it," until the dog moves steadily ahead, nose down. Then straighten up. Walk beside dog quietly, as long as he keeps working.

When he comes to the second article, praise him heartily if he noses it or picks it up. If he ignores it, say, "Oh, look! See this great thing!", pick it up and tease him with it; praise him as soon as he tries to take it. Then pocket the article, say "Go find another one. Track it," and point again to the trail.

Handling on Turn. Approaching the turn, take a firm grip on the lead. If the dog is moving rapidly, restrain him enough to slow him down, but don't discourage him. Many dogs will keep their noses down and follow this slight turn perfectly with no assistance other than being slowed.

If the dog overruns the turn, either back up slightly until he is coming at it again from his original direction or stand still and give him lead enough to circle. It is normal for a dog's nose to come up when he loses the ground track and for it to drop when he passes over the track in his circle. Instantly encourage him, "Track it!" and go with him. You may have to repeat this two or three times before he gets it right. If he noses down the new leg of the track and heads the proper way, go with him even if he cut the exact corner.

Second Leg. Continue as before to the third article (the end). If the dog moves steadily, nose down, you can drop back a few feet behind him. Hold back ever so slightly on lead, gradually increasing the pressure until he understands the correct thing is to pull you along (an obedience-trained dog that has been taught not to forge may be slow to comprehend this, so NEVER attach a tracking lead to his collar except to walk the dog to start).

Praise at each find must be enthusiastic and physical--hug your dog, kiss him, play with him, convince him he's the greatest. Praise is what turns the shy, tentative "find" into a proud, confident one. Some dogs revel in carrying the last article back home. Reward him for any indication at all, even a single sniff or pause. Then mark your map.

Repetition. Do two or four of these short tracks a day for your first week. If one contains a right turn, the next should contain a left turn, to avoid developing a preferred direction. Should your dog show a natural preference, do three tracks, with the extra turn in the non-preferred direction. At first, all tracks on any one day should be laid by the same person; later, the dog can track several different people successively without getting confused.

THINGS TO THINK ABOUT

1. Does the dog notice the first article? Does he connect its scent with the track? Does he increasingly keep his nose down and proceed eagerly?

2. Does the dog hesitate to start tracking again after finding an article? Could there be a scent pool around the article?

3. Does the dog stray to one side or the other of the track? Is this related to wind direction at ground- or nose-level? Are they the same?

4. Did the dog lose the scent at any point? If so, why? Is a puddle or wet log (scent collector) nearby? Is the track in a hollow (scent pool)?

5. What signs does this dog give of scent loss? Of making a find? Does he show a reaction to getting a whiff of article scent before the actual find? Such a reaction (an abrupt pause, a sniff skyward, a bark) is called an "alert."

LESSON 2 - MULTIPLE TURNS

When your dog is doing well on the Lesson 1 track (usually after the second or third week), add two more turns, placing a scent article a few paces after each. The track should still be laid 4 to 24 hours before running. Vary the turn angles and directions: right, left, sometimes alternating--don't let the dog learn a pattern. Never run the same, identical sequence twice in the same day. As before, study your map before running so that you know where the track should be.

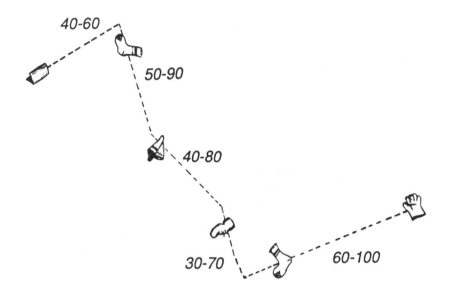

By now your dog should be moving right along, nose down. Drop back three or four paces behind; gradually increase your tension on the lead until the dog is actually pulling you. If the dog veers right or left of the track, tighten up on the lead. The farther off he gets, the more you should hold him back. As he tends to return to the track, gradually give him more lead, so that when he is on the track, you are following him readily at what you decide is your best "working tension." Each dog is different; try various tensions until you find one that assures him you are following but does not impede his progress.

Lead handling will take some practice, which may best be done away from your dog so he is not misled by your errors. Have a family member hold the end of the lead behind the center of his back with both hands and walk in front of you, veering to one side or the other until you get the knack of tightening a little to straighten him out, slackening as he gets back in line, stopping entirely if he goes far wrong or stops. If you're doing it right, it should feel as if you have power steering, or are neck-reining a horse. Note that this is a training device to get the dog working close on the track; it should never be done in a tracking test or on a real search, so don't make it a habit--always be conscious of doing it, and phase it out as you progress.

Be especially careful **not** to steer the dog on turns. If he overshoots a corner or turns the wrong way, stop dead. Encourage him, saying something like, "Good boy! Work it out." The dog should think you don't know where the track went. After he commits himself, go with him and resume your working tension.

Keep a close eye on your dog. Look at the tracklayer's map before starting and make a mental picture of it so that you are not fumbling for the map when you should be watching for signs of track loss or recovery. Your memory will grow more specific with practice as the tracks are more complex. Mark on the map what the dog did immediately after you praise his last find.

THINGS TO THINK ABOUT

1. Does the dog generally maintain a steady pace forward, nose down? Don't drop back behind him until he does.

2. Does the dog weave from side to side of the track? Apply the lead-handling tips given above. Or use numerous scent articles so he'll miss some if he strays; when you see him start to pass one up-wind, increase the lead pressure until he can't go forward and must either stand still or arc back onto the track with his nose right over the article. Say, "Oh, did you miss one? See, there it is! Good dog!" Give him much praise for getting back on the track, as if you had nothing to do with it.

3. What signs of track loss does this dog give besides ceasing to pull and raising his head?

4. What signs does the dog give of scenting an article? Wagging his tail? Stiffening his tail? Raising his ears? Wiggling his nose? "Pointing"?

5. At a turn, does the dog show a preferred direction--does he tend to try right, or left, regardless of where the track lies? Lay tracks with extra turns the **other** way. Does the dog tend to circle clockwise or counterclockwise when seeking to regain a lost track? Note this fact for future use.

LESSON 3 - PARTIALLY CONCEALED ARTICLE

Now that the dog is working well on a multi-turn, multi-article trail about 4 to 12 hours old, we make things harder. We run a track only 2 hours after it was laid. There has been discussion (Johnson, pp. 48-55) of a "hump" in the dog's learning that may appear when tracks aged between 30 and 60 minutes are attempted for the first time. The theory is that "body scent" and "track scent" are of equal strength at this age; the body odor predominates at first and declines rapidly toward zero while the disturbed earth-crushed vegetation scent comes to be stronger by virtue of its slower decline. Johnson conquers this problem with paired tracks laid 10 minutes apart but run successively, each day's pair being 5 minutes older than that of the day before. We do just the opposite; we start out with an older track and jump down to a fresher one. In our approach, many dogs show no signs of a hump, so we partially bury the second or third article to give them a challenge. Some dogs quit working unless given new problems often.

The same configurations as for Lesson 2 should be used; we are not seeking great endurance--yet. For the first try at a partially-concealed article, drop grass, pine needles, or other loose ground cover on it, leaving visible only one corner, or the end of a piece of surveyor's tape. (This tape is available at sporting goods stores, but is also carried by many hardware and feed stores at cheaper prices. You may need to tie tape onto your articles if you work in public areas, to make sure the dog is picking up the article with the tracklayer's scent and not something left by a skier or picnicker). On successive tries, increase the depth and density of the cover, until the dog will detect an article buried at least a foot under earth, gravel, or snow and will dig for it.

THINGS TO THINK ABOUT

1. Do you see any signs of a "hump"--evidence of confusion, frustration, or difficulty on this younger track? If so, does it seem influenced by temperature, humidity, time of day, wind conditions, ground cover? (Yes, you should be tracking under as varied conditions as possible.)

2. On the partially-buried article, does the dog seem to sniff the exposed portion before pulling it out? If so, or if dog shows signs of puzzlement, progress to a fully-buried article in very small steps.

3. When you reach the "fully-buried" stage, watch as you gradually increase the depth and density of the cover for signs of a limit on your dog's ability to detect the article. If present, is the limit affected by weather?

4. Does the dog start to circle, snuffling the ground, as he approaches the article? This indicates he essentially caught a whiff of it carried by close-to-ground air scent, the equivalent of the body-scent pool that forms around a stationary victim. Don't correct the dog. This short-range air

scenting can save you in a formal tracking test; if your dog is a little off and there happens to be an article coming up, the article scent pool can draw him back onto the trail. Air scenting disqualifies you only if the dog "cuts" one or more legs of the track to go directly to the article.

5. Does the dog dig eagerly? If not, bury a treat inside the article next time. To wean the dog from treats after his interest in articles is established, use a treat every other time, then every third time, then randomly. When there is no treat, praise extra hard.

6. When the dog is finding buried articles well, have the tracklayer place one or two up on a rock or a tree branch about shoulder-height. Does the dog snuffle around but seem unable to locate the source of the scent? You may have to go to him and, when his nose comes up, say, "Good dog, yes, here it is," while you ostentatiously pull the article down to him. After this first try in which you demonstrate to the dog that things can be up in the air as well as underfoot, he will not need such help again. Expect to see him jump into the air or try to climb the tree or rock to reach the article. (Caution: after you teach the dog things can be up high, don't expect him any longer to ignore flags placed in trees for your benefit. You may just have to stop relying on markers and start trusting your dog (see Lesson 5).

LESSON 4 - PERSON HIDING AT END OF TRACK

Now we jump to the other side of Johnson's hump--we use an absolutely fresh, just-laid track. On such a track, wind direction is important. Have your tracklayer walk the first leg with the wind at his back, so that the dog will first encounter the **points** of the scent cones fanning out from articles and clumped particles along the track, rather than the wide ends. This tends to keep the dog moving in a straight line instead of weaving from side to side (quartering). Also, the scent particles are densest in the air just above the point sources (the tracks and articles); thus, these points in the ground trail will stand out in the ribbon of air-borne body scent better than the diffuse ends of the cones and help the dog keep his sense of direction through the pool.

The tracklayer should walk the second leg with the wind off his right or left shoulder. By the third leg, your dog should have adapted to the air scent hanging along the track and learned to ignore it.

After dropping the final article, the tracklayer should hide about 10 paces downwind behind a tree, bush, rock, or other place of concealment. You should wait 5 minutes or count to 500 before starting, rather than have the tracklayer call out that he is ready and give the dog an audio direction cue (a call by radio is all right because it is directionless).

Run the track in the usual way, readying yourself for the dog's reaction when he comes onto the edge of the scent pool surrounding the tracklayer. This reaction is called an "alert". Different dogs show an alert in different ways, so you must learn what **your** dog's alert looks like. Your reaction to the alert should be to say, "Good dog. Check it out."

If your dog wants to charge directly into the hiding place after his alert, give him enough line and let him go, even if it means allowing him to skip the last article. However, if he does this, take him back to the article after you and the tracklayer have both praised him for the find and let him see what he missed. Do not treat him for the article unless he found it himself.

When the dog enters the hiding place, the tracklayer should first praise, then say "Go find (your name)" or "Go bring help". The dog should return to you; this is referred to as a "recall." Watch carefully to detect what sign he gives that he has found someone. Say, "Show me," and get him to lead you to the tracklayer; this is called a "refind." It should be done on lead at first, but after a few successful tries, you can start removing the lead when the dog indicates that he has scented a person.

THINGS TO THINK ABOUT

1. Did the dog show any signs of difficulty on the fresh track? If he has run loose and hunted, he probably won't, but otherwise the lingering pall of body scent could confuse him. If so, shorten up on the lead and increase

your working tension so that the dog must trail more slowly--essentially, you want him to drop back into a step-by-step (tracking) mode if he has moved up to a sniff-every-few-paces (trailing) mode.

2. Did the dog swing from side to side, as if going from one limit of the body scent path to the other? Increase the lead tension; the dog will tend to straighten out, keep his nose down, and work closer to the actual track.

3. Did you see the dog's alert? How did it differ from his reaction upon scenting an article? Try having the tracklayer recline, sit, or climb a tree. Is there a difference in the dog's alert under these circumstances?

4. Does the dog return to you promptly and take you to the tracklayer ("recall" and "refind")? On the next try, have the tracklayer pretend to be unconscious. Does the dog still come for back you without a command or cue? Great! You are ready to try some trailing off lead.

5. Having reached the level described in question 4 above, on your next attempt scent your dog on the article as usual but do not snap the lead onto the harness. Just give your "Track it" command and let the dog go. Does your dog range out about the length of the lead, as he has become accustomed? (Most will; then they will pause to make sure you are following at the usual distance, or even sit down and wait.) If your dog works too fast and starts to get farther ahead than you can see clearly, give the command, "Wait up." When you have regained your working distance, say, "All right. Good boy! Track it." If this goes well, do some future exercises on-lead and some off-lead, but be sure you retain the dog's willingness to work on-lead for those circumstances where it would endanger him to be loose (along the shoulder of a freeway, for instance).

LESSON 5 - LOCATING A BLIND TRACK

So far, you have known where the track was that you wanted the dog to follow. Now you will proceed to work blind tracks and must learn to trust your dog.

Have the tracklayer choose two markers 50 to 100 paces apart as shown below, then walk in a straight line perpendicular to the imaginary line joining the markers until he crosses it and is at least 20 paces beyond.

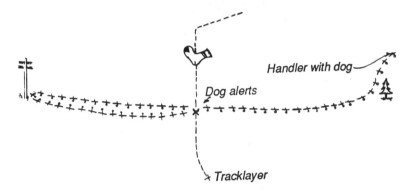

At that point he should drop the first article and proceed to lay a track of 5 or 6 legs and an equal number of articles, making some of the legs as much as 250 paces long. (From this lesson onward, at least once a week run a progressively longer track until your dog can easily cover a mile or more.) The tracklayer should map only the part that comes after the first article.

Take the dog, on lead, to the first marker. Tell him, "Take scent." Point at the imaginary line between the two markers, and move along it with him. Watch carefully; when he noses down, say excitedly, "That's it, that's it!" and shift the lead from his collar to his harness. Give your "Track it" command, let him make his turn and move out in front. After a few paces he will find the article, and this will tell you the direction he took was correct (there is no article off the other direction). Proceed as with previous tracks.

If you reach the second marker without the dog's giving any track sign, turn around and go back toward the first marker. Some dogs seem to notice they have crossed a track much better the second time they encounter it-- they probably scented it the first time but did not indicate it because they felt unsure of themselves. Have someone watch you; a subtle track alert is more easily seen from farther away.

When you get onto one or more of the long legs shown on your map, the dog may start working with his head higher, or lower his nose for a sniff of the ground and then go on with it held high for several steps. He will appear to be checking the ground scent off and on rather than constantly.

Do not object to this unless he begins moving far off to one side or the other--what he has done is to shift to the trailing mode. You will want to use it for long searches.

In subsequent sessions, have the tracklayer leave progressively more legs out of the map he gives you until you are running the whole track completely blind. Now you are ready for a real search.

THINGS TO THINK ABOUT

1. Did you recognize the dog's track alert without help? How does it differ from his article alert and his people alert? If you saw it only as you headed back toward the first marker, is it possible he did alert on the initial pass and you didn't see it?

2. Following the dog's track alert, were you confident he was on the right trail before you saw the article? Is the dog's tracking posture different when you know where the trail is, compared with when you don't know? If so, you are telegraphing your guess about the trail to the dog, and you must break him from relying on you. One method is to deliberately cue him in the wrong direction and praise him when he insists on the right one--cue him straight ahead where you know there's a turn, or vice versa. He's more apt to insist on his own way if you miscue him just at an article scent pool.

CAUTION: For the dog with a strong obedience background, make the first miscues very subtle and only on an overridingly clear track or almost on top of the article. It will really shake this dog up to learn you can be wrong! He must be absolutely sure he is right and you aren't--then give quick, quick praise for his cleverness. If your timing isn't that good, it may be easier to train yourself to stop telegraphing than to train the dog to stop looking to you.

3. As you work from a map with more and more blind legs, does your confidence in the dog grow? Is he reliable, or does he sometimes lead you wrong? Are there signs in his tracking posture that he is leaving the track? That he is not sure of himself? That he has totally lost the scent?

4. Do you detect an abrupt shift to the trailing mode, or is the dog drifting into it so gradually you hardly notice? Does he shift back to step-by-step tracking on occasion? Is there a change in his working speed when he shifts to trailing?

5. Repeat with tracks aged 12 to 24 hours, not aged at all, and everywhere in between. Does the dog's tracking posture on a fresh track differ from that on an old one? Do you see any signs of Johnson's "hump"? What changes occur in your dog's tracking style when the weather is wet? When it is very dry? When the wind is strong? When the air is still?

LESSON 6 - DISCRIMINATION: DOUBLE CROSSTRACK

This is our first exercise in scent discrimination. If it sounds difficult, remember that unless you work on very isolated grounds, you have already run tracks under- and overlaid with a wide variety of crosstracks--you just were not aware of them. Your dog undoubtedly was, however.

Have your tracklayer put out a track 3 to 4 hours before you intend to run it. At two points in the track, have him set a flag with each hand so that you have flags 5 to 6 feet apart with the trail midway between. Two hours after the main track is laid, have the crosstrack layers enter the area at one side, map in hand. They should walk side by side, about 4 to 6 feet apart, keeping the flags in line as they approach so as to cross the track perpendicularly. They should cross it each place where they see a pair of flags (walking parallel to the line joining the pair, one on each side of it), and exit the area without coming closer than 30 paces to any other part of the main track. On the first try, have them leave the flags so you will know where to watch for your dog's crosstrack indication; subsequently, have them pick up the flags.

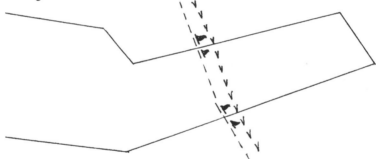

Paths of the crosstrack layers relative to the main track.

Run the track as you have the previous ones. Ideally, your dog should indicate the presence of the crosstracks but continue on the main track. He may pause at each person's trail, look one way and then the other, then go on straight ahead. He may even take a step or two in each direction. Your part is to stand quietly until dog commits himself...and this means 15 or 20 steps. Though many excellent dogs act as if the crosstrack were not there at all, it is reassuring to the handler to get a clear crosstrack indication. If the dog either alerts differently to a crosstrack than to a scent he was given, or merely alerts twice a few feet apart, the handler has no doubt about whether it's a crosstrack or a corner as long as he keeps his patience. If the dog ignores the cross- tracks, however, it isn't worth the effort to teach him to alert on them; just add that fact to your knowledge of how the dog works.

You don't need many of these--only enough to learn what your dog's crosstrack indication, if any, looks like. Possible elaborations are: (a) using a single crosstrack layer; (b) laying the crosstracks at a low angle to the basic track; (c) having the crosstrack layers turn and walk along the basic track for 10 or 15 paces before turning again and going off in their original direction. If that doesn't confuse your dog, nothing will.

Run enough of these to make **you** feel secure with unflagged crosstracks. The chances are your dog has been detecting and routinely ignoring them from the day you started training.

THINGS TO THINK ABOUT

1. What does the dog do, if anything, when he comes to a set of crosstracks? If your dog forges ahead on the main track without pause, that's fine for AKC work. An active searcher, though, may want to know if someone is out there besides himself and the victim. Lesson 9 tells how to get your dog to indicate a crosstrack.

2. If the dog gives a crosstrack signal, how does it differ from his "found trail" indication? (The difference may be subtle.)

3. Does he indicate both crosstrack layers' paths, or only that something disturbed the trail at this point? What happens when a car or truck crosses the trail instead of people walking?

4. Let the original tracklayer be one of the crosstrack layers, but be sure to preserve a two-hour difference in time. Does the dog indicate the crosstracks differently from in the preceding exercise? If not, do you think the dog is unable to distinguish individual scent--or does the time differential make it a "new track" to him? How will this affect a trail doubling on itself? (Don't repeat this more than once because its only purpose is to enlighten you; it teaches the dog nothing.)

NOTE: Do not attempt to change whatever the dog does on this; simply note whether he stays with the main track or goes with the fresher trace of the main tracklayer. If the former, you have a dog who "plays the game" once he knows what it is, and you can lay both main track and crosstracks yourself in future practices. Otherwise, be sure to have one or the other laid by some different person.

LESSON 7 - MULTIPLE TRACKLAYERS

You will need two tracklayers for this. Have them each leave an article at the start and walk together for a hundred yards or so. Then have them plant a flag or other marker and have one take off to the right, the other to the left. A few paces after their paths divide, each should drop an article, then proceed as if laying a normal track. After each has dropped one more article, he should hide 20 or 30 paces beyond.

Start the dog by having him "Take scent" on one person's article. Carry the article with you in a plastic bag (turn the bag inside out, insert your hand, grasp the article through the material of the bag, turn the bag right side out leaving the article inside and your hand outside, then put a twist-tie on the top). When you come to the marker, work out the first track the dog tends to follow until you find the person. Ask him if the article you've been working the dog on was his. If so, return to the marker and work out the other track, saying ,"Go find the other one." Be careful not to let the dog backtrack the double track to the start. Realize that your dog knew there were two tracks all along. If he seems reluctant to start on the second person's trail, take him to the article dropped after the trails divide (which should be visible from the marker) and restart him there.

If the wrong person was found, have him return with you to the marker and hide again, starting at a different angle from the marker than either of the first two trails and leaving an article close to where he turns off. Meanwhile, have your dog find the person who dropped the article from which he originally took scent. Re-scent him first at the marker, on the article you have been carrying, then if necessary on the article visible from the division point.

After your dog finds the person he began searching for, take him back to locate the person who has re-hidden. This is a very important exercise. If family members are lost together, the strongest is apt to tell the others to stay put while he goes for help and then, frightened or tired of waiting, they wander off in separate directions. The dog must learn to finish finding one, then look for another--some dogs will run back and forth frantically between the various tracks until totally confused and end up finding nobody.

In a class, this exercise can be done with two dogs at a time. Have each tracklayer use a matched pair of gloves or socks for the start and for the drop shortly after the marker. Each dog is scented on one of the articles at the start, and when the handlers come to the marker that shows where the tracklayers separated, they will know if their dogs have chosen the correct branch of the trail to follow by seeing if the article a short way down the branch matches the one they are carrying. This is a very good exercise for training two dogs from the same household to work independently.

THINGS TO THINK ABOUT

1. Did the dog seem confused when the trails separated? Did he tend to choose one even before you scented him on the article? Why?

2. Did the dog find the correct person for the first article? If you were tracking a lost child and parent and you had visible tracks to go by, which trail would you scent the dog on first? Why? (You will want to locate the one who can be found sooner because he cannot travel as fast and is more likely to need physical assistance before devoting your efforts to finding the more able member of the pair.)

3. After the dog has found both people correctly a time or two, try not scenting the dog on the second person's article after the first find; just say "Go find the other one." Does this work when you have the first person with you? Does it also work when you don't?

4. Try this with trails aged two to four hours, and articles instead of people at the ends. Can the dog match up the articles correctly? (If one person drops warm-colored articles and the other cool-colored articles, you will never be in doubt that your dog is sticking to the correct trail even if they cross and re-cross several times. The latter is an advanced exercise; its practical application is to the case where one person is pursuing another, often losing the trail and having to cut back and forth to find it again. Your assignment could be either to find and detain the pursuer before he overtakes the pursued, or else to locate the pursued as speedily as possible because he may be in the early stages of hypothermia and irrationally trying to elude another rescuer, whom you can contact on your way back.)

LESSON 8 - SCENT POOLS AND OBSTACLES

A scent pool will tend to form around any person (or object) that remains in a fixed spot. It will spread outward, as a circle on flat ground with no wind; as an ellipse on flat ground with a steady wind; as an irregular blob following ground or vegetation contours in a gulley or glen. A scent pool may or may not be an obstacle: we have seen it help beginning dogs find articles and pull them back onto the trail; we have also seen it bewilder TDX dogs right at the starting stake.

Another condition that is generally an obstacle is a change in the ground surface, an interface between tracking media. Most blatant, of course, is the change from soft earth to bare pavement or a rock outcrop-- these hold scent only in small depressions, weeds growing from cracks, or sticks and other debris lying on the surface. Going from bare soil onto grass, from a clearing onto forest floor covered with pine needles, from gravel onto plowed furrows, can be equally disconcerting. The track scent changes quality, and the dog may not recognize it for the same trail at first. The only way a dog learns about scent obstacles is by experience with them.

Work with your tracklayer to design a trail that goes over bare rock or paving, across a clearing in thick woods, from a grassy field into freshly plowed earth, up or down a creek bed for 50 paces or so, through a relatively round hollow and later across a gulley, etc. Run these tracks in the usual way, ageing the first ones at least overnight and the later ones an hour or less. Record the results in each case.

THINGS TO THINK ABOUT

1. Did you see confusion or loss of track when the dog crossed the interface from one ground cover to another? If so, do many interfaces, reassuring the dog that it is the same trail even though it smells different in many ways. Not all dogs find media change to be a problem.Some have conquered it chasing rabbits. Others learn how to handle it when they work the aged tracks, where the effects are noticeable but not extreme, before being confronted with the odor of crushed vegetation, exposed moist earth, and heavy air scent on the very fresh track. If your dog appears to track steadily right over interfaces on tracks aged an hour or less, proceed to some other problem.

2. Did the bare rock or paving have cracks, depressions, puddles, weeds growing up through holes, damp trash lying around? Did the dog use all these scent repositories? To get him to notice them, expose him to them one at a time, if possible--by limiting his options, you direct dog's attention to the few scent sources that remain.

3. If total track loss occurs at an obstacle, such as a paved highway, take the dog directly across, then encourage him to search up and down

the far edge. This also works for gullies unless the edges are too irregular. Does the dog's head drop as in initially finding the trail (see Lesson 6)?

4. Try this on a flowing creek: direct the tracklayer to walk in the water some 50 paces upstream at one point and downstream at another. Cross perpendicularly where the trail enters the water, then search up and down the shore for its emergence. Does the dog's behavior show whether the tracklayer was walking upstream or downstream before he enters the water? Is the dog's indication for a barefoot tracklayer different from that for one wearing rubber boots? Can you tell from dog's actions whether tracklayer was or was not in the creek at a particular point?*

5. At a round hollow, or where the TDX starting stake is in the middle of a clearing, or where you must start from a canteen the victim has dropped, try walking the dog around the outside of the area. Does his nose go down? Go all the way around again; if the dog's nose drops at the same place, allow him to take that trail. Be sure your circle is large enough to fall outside the edge of the scent pool. Do you see now why we have not encouraged the dogs to backtrack? We almost always want them to take the trail in the forward direction.

---

* On a real search at San Felipe Pueblo in 1985, my dog was asked to verify that the victim was still in the Rio Grande downstream past the pueblo boundary. The dog did so indicate. Five or six weeks later, the body washed up against a dam on the north end of Albuquerque.

LESSON 9 - DISCRIMINATION PROOFING

In Lesson 6, your dog learned not to be fooled by a double cross-track laid after the main trail. Now have a single crosstrack layer walk across the area **before** the main trail is laid and drop a decoy article bearing his scent near a landmark you have preselected for your main trail. (This article should be bright-colored and placed in the open where you can see it coming up as you run the trail.) Except for the article, most dogs will not see this as a new problem; all your tracks were unquestionably crossed and recrossed by numerous people and animals, whether you knew it or not.

After an hour or more, have the main track laid. To keep this interesting for dogs who discriminate from instinct or early experience, have one article buried and another stuck in a bush at about the dog's shoulder level. The main trail should pass about five to ten paces from the decoy, and should cut the crosstrack at least twice. Then the tracklayer should join several people chatting in the parking area while you run the track. At this stage, you know only the starting point, how many "true" articles are to be found, and the general whereabouts of the decoy (preferably, you **don't** know who laid the track).

Run the trail as usual, collecting the true articles. At the decoy, if your dog alerts, goes to it, or sniffs it, that is all right, but use your "Leave it!" command if he starts to pick it up. Praise him when he returns to the correct trail. As he approaches the group in the parking area, increase your lead tension and tell your dog ,"Find him/her!", offering one of the true articles if the dog will sniff it (many dogs are impatient at being re-scented while on a "live" trail). The dog should go to the person who laid the main track.

THINGS TO THINK ABOUT

1. Does the dog ignore the crosstrack and the decoy article? Make a note of it in the dog's record, but don't try to change this behavior. There is no good reason why a dog should alert on irrelevant signs **older** than the track he is running.

2. Does the dog appear distracted from the main trail--do the decoy and crosstracks make him nervous? If so, you should alternate the first part of this track with a Lesson 6 track until your dog not only is consistently right about what is the main trail but chooses it with an air of assurance.

3. Does the dog want you to notice the decoy but then seem eager to proceed with the main trail when you have acknowledged it? This is the ideal case. Note it in the dog's record, and remember any difference you saw between his indication of the decoy and his indication of true articles.

4. Would you have known the decoy article was not a true one by the dog's behavior even if it had not been a conspicuous color? (His either totally ignoring it or indicating it differently counts as a "yes".)

5. What does your dog do if the crosstrack and the main track are laid almost simultaneously, three hours prior to running? Does it make a difference if one tracklayer weighs considerably more than the other? (If you are interested in the theory behind tracking methods, read Johnson pp. 43-47 and compare with your results. Study Johnson's use of the term "body odor" carefully. How does it resemble/differ from "individual track scent" as used in this training guide?)

6. Was the dog's approach to the tracklayer in the group positive and happy, or did it seem tentative? If the latter, run more Lesson 4 tracks to be sure the dog is not surprised at finding a person at the end of the trail, then do this again. Can you tell whom the dog will select before he picks him out? How far off is the dog when he becomes sure whom he is looking for? If you were tracking someone who had robbed a jewelry store, would you be positive enough that this was the man to have him searched?

LESSON 10 - DROP TRAILING

This exercise requires two vehicles and drivers in addition to a tracklayer. Ask the tracklayer to start off as an ordinary trail, but on the third leg come to the edge of the road. The first vehicle, waiting down the road, will pull up, take the tracklayer in, and drive on about a quarter of a mile. The tracklayer will then get out, drop a scent article by the road, lay two more legs, and hide in a bush.

Start to run this track the usual way, but have the second vehicle waiting where the driver can see you signal. Wave to him when the dog comes to the road and indicates loss of track. Enter the second vehicle--if it is a pickup, you and the dog get in back; otherwise, you sit in the center of the front seat with the dog by the partially open window (you **can** do this with one driver if you leave the dog on a Stay while you go get the vehicle parked downroad, but never use the vehicle the tracklayer was in to search for him). Have the driver proceed slowly along the road while you watch the dog, who will probably have his nose out the window and tilted up. If his nose turns down, or the dog starts barking or scratching at the glass, stop, get out, and give the dog your "Find scent" command. This should be the point where the tracklayer left the first car. Run the trail to its conclusion.

If the dog gives no indication over the segment of road where the tracklayer could have taken off again, have the driver turn around and go back the other way. Still no indication? Repeat while watching more closely; most dogs' indications are vigorous, even desperate, but your dog's might be subtle. (Do make sure the dog is not sitting over the vehicle's exhaust).

THINGS TO THINK ABOUT

1. Did the dog give a clear indication of where to stop? (Most dogs will.) Repeat, but do not have the tracklayer drop an article where he leaves the vehicle. Does the dog still indicate where the vehicle should stop to put him back on trail? This can be done with boats, having the tracklayer dive out; be prepared for dog to try to jump overboard or, if scared of the boat's rocking, he may lean over and seem to bite the water, or raise his muzzle and howl.

2. Did the dog indicate no stopping point at all, going either direction on the road? Possibly he thought the exercise was over when he got into the car. Drive back and forth again; scent the dog on the article and keep saying, "Find him" while encouraging him to test the air outside the window. (If you've taught the dog not to stick his head out, you'll need to overcome that conditioning.) Still no luck? Call the tracklayer in and have him hide in a ditch or bush right at the point where he left the road. Have the vehicle driven close to his hidingplace at a very slow speed, allowing a few minutes

for a scent pool to form around the tracklayer. Once the dog finds the tracklayer beside the road, he will know the trail is only temporarily lost if a subject gets into a car and will then find articles and even the bare track easily. (This is the kind of thing the dog can learn completely in one experience.)

3. Repeat, but have the first vehicle sitting empty on the road at which the tracklayer aims the first part of the trail. The tracklayer gets in, drives a quarter or half mile, abandons the vehicle beside the road, and cuts across country. Does the dog indicate the first vehicle--which seat the tracklayer occupied, which door he used?

4. Will this work on a highway? Try it on a not-too-busy stretch, keeping the dog on a strong lead, particularly when he is inside the vehicle (a dog can push windows down!)

AIR SCENT

LESSON PLAN

Equipment for air scent work:

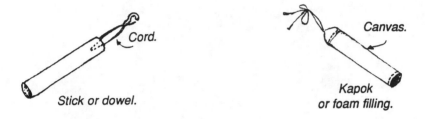

Stick or dowel.   *Cord.*   *Canvas.*   *Kapok or foam filling.*

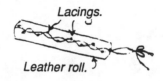

Lacings.

Leather roll.

Some possible designs for bringsels.

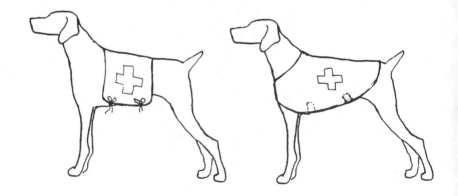

Two types of shabrach design .

AIR SCENT LESSON PLAN

Normally, you will want to start air scent after your dog masters tracking/trailing. The dog without prior experience more easily relates scent on an object to scent on the ground (both lack the lighter molecules of the identifying scent profile) than scent from an object (dominated by heavier molecules) to an airborne scent (dominated by lighter molecules). The handler more easily learns to read a dog on a line 20 to 40 feet ahead than a dog bounding 50 or 100 yards ahead; and he obviously has more control of the dog's learning process. Moreover, dogs readily shift from the disciplined tracking mode to the freer air scent mode but may be unwilling to stop down their air scent to the rigors of tracking. If you want your dog eventually to do both, by all means start with tracking.

However, for those who want to teach **only** air scent, the first two lessons provide a way to get started. You will note the dog looks for a **particular scent** until he has learned that his task is to find a person from airborne traces; later he locates multiple subjects with no scent object as guidance and distinguishes a casual encounter from a "find".

The dog that already tracks should start as follows. Run a short track with three or four scent articles and the tracklayer hidden about 50 feet upwind of the last. When the dog finds this article, go to him and offer praise/treats. As the wind brings scent from the tracklayer to the dog, it is natural for his head to go up and his nose to turn toward the scent stream that resembles what he has just been tracking. When you see this, unsnap the lead and give your air scent command--"Go find!" or whatever. The dog runs to the tracklayer, you follow, and both reward the dog. Go to Lesson 3.

Materials needed. The air scent dog needs a well-fitted fabric or leather collar. For night work, an electric flasher or a reflective strip is helpful. Do not use an obedience slip collar because the rings tend to catch on obstacles. The handler should dress for wilderness hiking, with sturdy boots, and should always carry a canteen. At night, a good flashlight is needed, preferably a headlamp because it leaves your hands free. Two-way radios allow you to communicate with your subject(s) and your training base. A whistle gives you control of your dog at a greater distance; you may like a "silent" one with adjustable frequencies above the human audio range. (Some handlers put bells on their dogs, but in cover you'll find you can hear your dog moving for quite a distance without one and in the open you'll see him--so why add unneeded noise that might mask a call for help?)

You might wish to equip your dog with a "bringsel"--an object attached to his collar so that he can reach down, take it in his mouth, and carry it back to you to show that he has made a find. You can use a rolled up piece of leather, a stick with a hole in the end, or anything that hangs down far enough for the dog to grab it but won't catch on brush or bump the dog's legs. Soft objects are easier on the teeth. Some common types of bringsel appear on p. 66, and the use of the bringsel is explained in Lesson 3.

For cold weather work, the shorthaired dog may need a coat. It should be designed to cover the dog's chest and belly, the area that tends to get ice cuts as he bounds through crusted snow. A dog coat with a Velcro closure along the back is illustrated on p. 37. A set of boots will prevent ice accumulating between the toes and burrs or goatheads penetrating the pads, if you can get the dog to leave them on. Some field handlers encircle the dog's lower leg with plastic tape loosely enough not to impede circulation, then fasten the top of the boot to it with another strip that can be pulled off and reattached painlessly. Inasmuch as dogs perspire mostly through their feet, absorbent padding is advisable to keep the inside of the boots from getting clammy and also provide more insulation.

Just as the harness signals the dog to track or trail, so the coat cues him to air scent. When it is too warm for a coat--or if your dog is a breed that doesn't need such protection--you may wish to use a "shabrach" or vest. (see p. 66, bottom). Many teams put their insignia on the sides of the shabrach to furnish identification in the field as well as when traveling on public carriers that do not normally permit dogs. The shabrach should be well fitted, to slide smoothly through bushes and briers, and should be of a rugged but breathable fabric to permit air circulation. A shabrach that soaks up water can be used as a cooler in very hot weather.

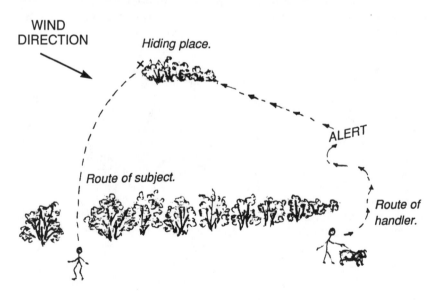

WIND DIRECTION

Hiding place.

ALERT

Route of subject.

Route of handler.

C-pattern with barrier, used to start the air scent dog.

LESSON 1 - STARTING A DOG ON AIR SCENT

Locate your first exercise in a fairly level, open area with spots of brush or trees for hiding places. Try to work at a time when the wind is steady and not too strong, sweeping down the open area toward your starting place (if the wind direction is wrong, go to a different boundary of the area).

The starting point should be downwind of a hedge, line of brush, or other scent barrier from the place you wish the subject to hide--a wall is ideal. Walk your dog to the start on lead. Your subject should accompany you, carrying a tuggie, chew toy, or other object from his own home that will hold his scent well. When you reach the place behind the barrier along the edge of your working grounds, let out some lead and request the subject to play vigorously with the dog, making sure he gets plenty of his scent on the toy. Now he should throw down the toy or hand it to you; then while you hold the dog close and block his view, the subject should run off around the end of the barrier to the prearranged hiding place.

When he is gone, pick up the toy in a plastic bag or wearing a plastic glove. The dog will learn to ignore your scent on objects, but at first make it easy by minimizing this distraction. Hold out the toy to the dog so he can't miss the scent on it and wave it to excite his curiosity: "Where is he? Where did he go?" You can even swing the toy out in front as if you were going to throw it as you take the dog around the other end of the barrier from the one the subject used. Move briskly; make it fun.

Once you are out from behind the barrier, the wind from the hiding place should bring the subject's scent to the dog. Watch for his head to go up and his whole body to tense, while his nose may wiggle or at least turn in the direction the wind is coming from. His tail may stiffen, or else it may wag furiously. This behavior is called an "Alert". While the signs differ with individual dogs, all show the basic quality of suddenly snapping to attention. Your response should be "Good boy--go find him. Check it out!" Drop the lead and let the dog run ahead of you to the hiding place. (If you already have good verbal control over your dog off lead, you can unsnap the lead and let him run free. However, at this early stage where he doesn't know exactly what the game is, an untrained dog may run off, and his dragging a long lead improves your chance of retrieving him.)

If the dog does not run out toward the hiding place ahead of you, then you must run beside him, encouraging him all the time to work up the scent cone toward the subject. Zigzag back and forth, so that the dog passes in and out of the scent cone--this focuses the dog's attention on it. As he becomes more intent on the scent cone, what with your encouragement and the fact that the scent grows stronger the nearer he gets to the subject, you can drop back behind him (actually, you may be unable to keep up as his eagerness increases). Do, though, continue excited verbal encouragement until he bursts into the hiding place and confronts the subject.

Both of you should praise the dog heartily. For the dog that responds to a "play" reward, throw the scent object/toy to the subject and let the dog tug on it or use it for a retrieving game. The food-oriented dog should be given a treat the subject has carried with him. Make this a very happy time, one the dog will remember with joy and seek to recapture. Return to the start side by side, with the dog running around you, to foster the idea that our purpose is to get everybody together. Much play with the toy and the subject will confirm the relationship already established between the airborne body scent and the scent imparted to the toy at the start. On subsequent tries, your Seek command should be given earlier and earlier, not waiting for the alert, until you leave the barrier with a hearty "Go find!" and use only the "Check it out!" to encourage the dog after the alert occurs.

THINGS TO THINK ABOUT

1. When he struck the edge of the scent path, what signs did your dog give? Did he stop dead? Stare upwind? Give a yelp? Leap in the air? Sometimes at first the alert is very tentative, even puzzled, but with lots of encouragement it will become more and more distinct.

2. Did the dog realize at once that this scent cone related to the person he played with earlier and the toy you are carrying with you? If not, one way to prompt his realization is to wave the toy under the dog's nose as he stands bewildered, trying to understand why this smell borne on the wind is intriguing. You can even prompt, "Is that him? Is it? Go find him!"

3. Did the dog work back and forth in a zigzag pattern from one edge to the other of the scent cone, the pattern growing tighter and tighter as the cone narrows on approaching the subject? Or did he zoom straight to the hiding place (presumably, down the center of the cone)? Either is fine, but you must recognize your dog's reaction to this scent pattern, so you will know it when you see it again.

4. What factors could interrupt your dog's pursuit of the scent cone? For each one, how can you best help the dog relocate the cone?

5. Was the dog enthusiastic at his first find, only to show a "Who cares?" attitude later? He may be getting bored. Resist the temptation to play the same game over and over on any one day. Go train at something else, and next time look for a different person, in a different place. Dogs differ greatly in their desire for variety; to some, three successive retrieves are pushing it, whereas others will retrieve the same ball or dummy all day.

LESSON 2 - FORMAL WORKUP; BEGIN REFIND

The next stage of air scent work dispenses with the preliminary play, but not with the scent object. Using a similar course layout, have the person you will seek drop a well-scented toy behind the barrier and go off to hide while the dog is still in the car. When he is in place, get the dog out and bring him to the start on lead. Make a big fuss over discovering the toy on the ground and work up the dog's interest: "Look here! What's this? Where's its owner? Let's go find him!" You can even use the words "Take scent" because the purpose of this workup is exactly the same as in scenting the dog to run a ground track.

When the dog is quivering with eagerness, run with him around the end of the barrier and give your "Go find!" command. If the dog dashes forward, drop the lead and follow. You can hang back a little, the better to observe how your dog discovers and works the scent cone, but don't get so far behind that the dog begins to think you're not still with him. Nothing destroys the dog's enthusiasm quicker than the suspicion you don't care about what he's doing.

It is desirable to have the dog some distance ahead of you when he crashes into the hiding place, because you must now do a little acting. You want the dog to return to you and take you to the subject--and why would he need to do that if you were only six feet behind? Advise the subject not to treat the dog at once, but instead to say, "Good dog. I need help. Go get (your name)." A dog that immediately starts back to the handler on his own doesn't need this command and should be allowed to go without comment.

If you want your dog to indicate his finds eventually with some sort of bringsel, give it to the subject before he goes to hide. When the dog arrives, the subject should fasten the string to the collar to avoid loss, put the bringsel gently in the dog's mouth and say, "Take it to (your name)."

When you hear the subject talking to your dog (who is out of your sight in the bushes), call "(Dog's name), come!" Be quite persuasive: this dog expects his play/praise right after the find. When he does come (with or without a bringsel), praise him enthusiastically and pick up the lead: "Good dog! Did you find him? Show me! Take me to him!" Let the dog lead you to the subject, then both of you praise him and play with him.

Technically speaking, when the dog returned to you after finding the subject, he did a "recall." When he took you back to the subject, that was a "refind." Now all you have to do is polish the procedure.

There are some problems to overcome. A young or very submissive dog is apt to believe master knows everything and there's no real need for him to show you the find. You must convince him that without his help you could never find the subject.

You must recognize that dogs in a very emotional state don't think well.Some get so excited at making a find that they dash all over looking for you and never think to try scenting you or backtracking themselves to you. If this behavior occurs, call the dog's name, then step behind a tree so he must work to find you. Next time he'll keep track of you better.

A dog that is overjoyed at locating you again may forget where he left the subject. If this occurs, walk him zigzag on lead, repeating the "Show me" command until he either remembers or catches the scent again.

The bringsel presents problems of its own. The excitable dog or avid retriever may so love carrying a bringsel that he takes it in his mouth on the alert or even when you first send him out, so that it has no value as a signal. Having the subject keep the bringsel until he is discovered causes the dog to regard it as a post-find reward. If the dog should drop the bringsel before or as he reaches you, put it gently back in his mouth as you pick up the lead and have him carry it back to the subject.

Some dogs signal a find by returning with a stick off the ground, or the subject's hat or glove. One I know of returns and pulls a ball out of her handler's pocket to show a find. Two of mine will take my clothes in their teeth and pull me in the direction they want me to go.

Lacking a signal, you must be extremely attentive to your dog's body language: you must know when he has succeeded and when he is merely checking back to be sure you're still following. One cure for checking back (and for false alarms) is to put the dog on lead and demand he show you the find until he admits it was simply an attention-getting device. If you overreact to a mere alert, the dog may give false signals just to please you.

THINGS TO THINK ABOUT

1. Are you becoming confident that you recognize your dog's alert and find indications? Do they differ from those of your friends' dogs?

2. After the recall, is your dog eager to take you to the subject? To increase his motivation, have the subject show him a treat but withhold it until the dog returns with you. Or let the subject pretend to be injured; the dog's natural response is to fetch all-powerful you to the rescue.

3. How determined is your dog? Firm him up by pretending not to understand, then show great surprise and joy as his signal gets stronger. (Be careful not to exceed his tolerance for frustration. This varies from dog to dog, so don't persist to where yours becomes frantic or desperate.)

4. Under what circumstances would you ever direct your dog where to search? If you are forced to do this (to avoid total failure of a day's practice, for instance), why must you be very sure you're right and the dog is wrong? Remember, your partnership depends on mutual trust.

LESSON 3 - SEARCH PATTERNS, AUDIO SIGNALS

For this exercise, use an area you have worked before which the dog knows is a place people are apt to be found. To give you time to work on patterning, have the subject hide quite a long distance out from the start.

Because we are not going to offer a scent article, you must put extra effort into your preliminary workup. Get the dog's attention: "Want to find somebody? Let's go get 'em! Who's out here?" From the Lesson 2 problems, he knows what you want of him now and the lack of a particular scent focus will not inhibit him. By this time, he should be ready to work free of restraint, so unsnap his lead as you say, "All right! Go find."

If you plan to use a whistle, introduce it now. Immediately after your "Go find" command, while the dog is bounding eagerly forward, give two short, sharp toots on your whistle. This is the "Go out" signal commonly used for bird dogs, so you are being consistent when you use it the same way here.

Now you want to build a search pattern. Aim yourself generally upwind but angle toward the right or left boundary of the pre-arranged search area. Say "This way!" or give the same two toots and gesture or run in the new direction. The dog, out in front, will swing to cut you off. Just before he reaches the boundary, turn 90° and run toward the other boundary, repeating the verbal or whistle command to get his attention. Now he will swing the other way. This is called "quartering." After lots of practice, you can walk up the middle of the field, merely facing in the new direction each time you signal, and the dog will run a zigzag from edge to edge so that his nose will detect any scent cone that drifts into the area. If he can't see you when you whistle, he will turn 90° frontwards from habit.

The dog should not continuously check back. If you see his pace slacken and suspect he is about to turn, urge him on with a shout of "Aaall riiight!" or two long whistle blasts, one high, the other low. If you lose him in heavy cover, signal to let him know you're coming along. Eventually, you'll burst through cover knowing exactly where he'll show up.

Sometimes the dog may get too far ahead for you to see his alerts. Use a shout of "Waa-ait" or "Waait up", or else two long whistles with a rising inflection to slow him down. (Introduce this command with the dog on a 40-ft lead, then proof it in a large fenced yard.)

The last whistle signal you need is "Come in"--a long blast that starts high, drops in pitch, then rises again; just the reverse of the bosun's whistle as heard in the Navy and on "Star Trek". By judicious use of these signals, you can fully control your dog's pattern.

And where do you want him to go? That depends on the terrain, wind direction, and shape of the search area. The scent behavior you need to consider in laying out the search pattern is described in Chapter IV.

When you see the first alert, urge the dog to "Check it out" as before. The dog's signals may be less definite because he doesn't know exactly what scent he is looking for, so you must observe very carefully. On a long search, your dog may strike the scent cone, lose it again, and resume patterning to recover it. If you noted the first alert and can analyze the wind and terrain, you can employ your direction signals to put the dog in the most likely spot for recovery. Follow through with the find, recall, and refind as in Lesson 2; the "Come in" whistle can be used for the recall if still needed.

Should your dog overrun the pre-arranged hiding place and reach the end of the area without making a find, direct him back downwind in a zigzag, watching for him to snap around and alert toward his REAR. If he gets close to the hiding place but can't pin down its direction, work him in a circle around it, gradually decreasing the diameter until he is right on top of the subject (under some atmospheric conditions, the scent may go straight up.) Now that you can put your dog wherever you want him without specifically guiding him, you can materially improve his chances of making a find.

THINGS TO THINK ABOUT

1. Does it surprise you that the dog picks up whistle signals almost effortlessly? Consider the amount of time you have spent developing the partnership, and how much farther you can hear a whistle.

2. Did your dog's actions show he believed someone must be out there despite having no scent article? If not, go back to Lesson 2 and run a few more sessions to gain his trust. The dog must believe you will never say "Go find" without good reason.

3. Do you see how you control the overall pattern, but your dog controls the details?

4. Are you reading your dog's signals clearly? Test this by having a more experienced handler walk behind you and call out each sign so you will know if you have missed any. The subtler signs are often easier to detect from farther back. How do these signs differ from those the dog gives for a subject who has left a scent article?

LESSON 4 - UNEXPECTED SUBJECTS

When your dog is responding well to the work-up in familiar surroundings, it is time to move to a new area or a new part of the old one. Include more challenging environmental features--steep terrain cut by stream beds and other obstacles; hollows that will act as scent traps; thick woods interspersed with open places; picnic tables and camp sites with multiple aged smells. If local law permits working your dog off-lead in an area where hikers and joggers are frequent, you can use them as "unexpected subjects" (but make sure your dog is under good verbal control and be ready with a quick explanation). Otherwise, you must get two or three friends to walk through the area in addition to your chief subject, who will find a hiding place and remain stationary. The "casual visitors" should begin their pre-arranged pattern when they hear you doing your work-up if they don't have radios.

After the work-up and the "Go find" command, watch your dog closely. It may confuse him to come onto a subject so soon after the start, and to come on more than one at a time; his signals may be hard to read. If you don't know exactly where the subjects are, command "Show me" every time the dog comes back to you. It is much worse to ignore a possibly valid find than to call for a refind on a false alarm. By this time you should know your dog's signals well enough to make few mistakes: an alert calls for "Check it out" and a return calls for "Show me!" On these casual finds, you may want to do the refind on lead to avoid your dog's frightening a stranger.

Always praise your dog for a find, even on someone you weren't looking for (sometimes a casual visitor will have seen or found evidence of your true subject). Then say, "Find another one--find someone else," and set him off again. In subsequent sessions, have one person walk close behind you (for instance, to carry your radio) and gradually farther back until your dog learns to distinguish someone who is "with you" from someone "to be found." If you are working toward membership in an organization that has performance tests, practice with several people up to 100 yards behind so that your dog learns to ignore the evaluators.

The alert and find indications on your chief subject should be easier. The find may occur at greater distance because the scent pool is larger and and the dog's refind will be more confident because the subject will stay put Therefore, let your dog work off-lead, being ready with a "Wait up" command in case he gets too far ahead of you. It's all right for him to run back and forth between you and the subject, but if he persists in running off, you might work him on a 40-ft lead until that separation becomes a habit (the number of repetitions required will vary with the dog). Maintain motivation by redoubling the praise after a difficult refind.

THINGS TO THINK ABOUT

1. Is your dog's natural search pattern different in this unfamiliar area? In what way?

2. Does your dog adapt his working range to the terrain and cover? You can encourage him to do so by using your "Wait up" command when he disappears from sight in heavy brush and your "Go out" command when the ground is more open. Note that when your dog is working at, say, 40 yds instead of 100 yds to either side, you will have to zigzag back and forth so that as a team you cover the same width-- your forward motion will take more time, but your search of the area will be more thorough.

3. Are you using your eyes and ears to supplement your dog's nose? In heavy cover, the scent may be so hemmed in that the dog must almost step on the subject to sense him. You should personally look into crevices behind rocks and logs, hollows where trees have been uprooted, under the lower branches at the base of evergreens, into thickets. During practice sessions, if you spot the subject before the dog scents him, use your patterning commands to put the dog downwind of the hiding place and work him closer and closer to it until he makes the find--pretend you didn't even see the subject. Act totally dependent on the dog, but meanwhile, train yourself to be alert in case at some point a life may depend on you.

4. What differences were there in the dog's behavior toward casual subjects as compared with the "true" subject? Might these apply to casual hikers encountered on a search for a lost hunter? Does your dog react differently to a person walking on two feet than to a sitting or reclining person?

5. Are you reading your dog well enough to know at all times whether he is pursuing his pattern, following out a scent clue, zeroing in on a subject, searching for you to notify you of a find (or to be sure he doesn't lose you), trying to guide you back to a subject he has located? Your ultimate success as an air scent team will depend on how well you read your dog.

6. If unusual weather occurred, how did it affect your dog's work? Many hunters claim their dogs cannot locate game if the wind is in the east (researchers qualify this by pointing out that east winds are very often storm winds, with associated turbulence and falling barometric pressure). Rain may wash scent into the ground, down runoff channels, or to deposition points far away from where it originated. Try to estimate to what extent unfavorable conditions degrade your dog's performance.

LESSON 5 - TWO-VICTIM EXTENDED SEARCH

For this exercise, you will use two "true subjects" and, again, an area of greater extent. The first or second session should be in open country, which will encourage the dog to increase the range of his pattern. If possible, use a topographical map to plan where the subjects will be hidden. One should be 500 paces or more from your starting point, the other about 750 paces out and at least 100 paces left or right from the first subject. Give them 15 minutes to hide before you begin to search.

Plan your search pattern to assure your dog's encountering the scent cone from the first victim, taking wind, humidity, terrain, and other conditions into account. Be ready for your dog's alert; quickly give your "Check it out" command. If he starts back to you and then gets wind of the second subject, do not permit him to check it out until he has led you to the first one--call or whistle him to you and put him on lead, if necessary. Note precisely where he alerted on the second subject; flag that spot with trail tape if you have some.

Complete the refind on the first subject; praise and reward your dog. Now take him (on lead if necessary) back to the marked spot where he alerted on the second subject, watching closely for another alert. If he did not alert on the recall or refind, work him upwind from the first find. Command, "Go find another one". Encourage the dog to increase the range of his pattern until he is working about 100 paces each side of your line of progress. When you see an alert, tell him "Check it out" and let him make the find. The first subject should stay right with you while you are doing this so that the dog does not become confused and try to "find" him again. When you have collected both subjects, give your dog extra praise. This division of interest is very hard for some dogs. The second and third tries will be easier, for the dog now realizes that his objective may be more than one person.

If your dog takes to finding two subjects readily, you may then wish to have him guide you all back to safety. Cast your dog loose and tell him, "Find the car" or "Let's go home." If he doesn't start back to the parking area, put him on a long lead and let him range out ahead while you direct him with your voice or whistle commands. Give him a special reward when you reach the car, and next time he will know what you mean by the "home" or "car" command. This is very useful if you are going into search work, for if you are wholly intent on your dog, you may not keep watch of your backtrail and in cloudy weather or in heavy cover where you can't get a compass fix on a landmark, finding the way back to the base camp or your vehicle can be a major problem.

THINGS TO THINK ABOUT

1. Did the dog seek out the second subject before completing the find on the first? You may have to repeat this exercise several times before it is clear to him that he must finish finding one person before he goes after another. When he has mastered finding two subjects confidently, increase the number of subjects to three or more.

2. Was there a difference in the dog's enthusiasm in seeking the two subjects? If he was **more** eager to find the second, all well and good; if he was **less** eager, you are not making the finds rewarding enough for him. Some people find it hard to let go and express delight, pride, joy, in terms their dogs can understand. Food will help with most dogs, but your attitude (or your ability to act) will have the greatest effect.

3. Are the refinds clear and distinct at this point? Does your dog show eagerness to get you to the subject? Is he now making allowance for your inability to move as fast as he--or follow him through stands of brush? If your dog shows impatience with you or tries to dart off on another search before you reach the subject, reduce the amount of praise you give when he recalls, and redouble the praise when he takes you to the find. Put him on leash as a last resort--your voice or whistle signals should give you firm control by this time.

LESSON 6 - EXTENDED SEARCH IN CHALLENGING TERRAIN; EVASIVE SUBJECT

This exercise needs to be laid out in terrain and cover that allow good hiding places for the subject. Its real life equivalent is the search for a small child who is afraid of being punished if found, or for a hypothermic or otherwise disoriented person who is unaware of his need to be rescued. Here are the general types of hiding places in ascending order of difficulty:

1. Above ground level--on top of a boulder, up a tree, on a roof. Airscent will scatter downwind from the hiding place.

2. At ground level but in a cave, a thicket, or on an island surrounded by vegetation (reeds, cattails, etc.) where the scent escaping is reduced to a mere trickle. A deserted building that lacks doors and windows may be used, but do not frustrate your dog with an airtight modern structure.

3. Below ground level--in a natural hole, an excavation, or a small hollow in snow or sand where scent escapes sporadically with turbulence or thermal stimulation.

4. Submerged, and covered with leaves, branches, or partially under snow (do not try complete burial in snow except in a regular avalanche rescue class due to the danger of suffocation). Scent will escape slowly, so the subject should hide at least 20 minutes before you start your search.

Only in the above-ground case will the dog succeed as readily as in our preceding exercises. If the air flow is not straight up, the scent pool from an elevated hiding place will be larger in radius than from one at ground level. This increases the dog's probability of encountering the pool but may complicate his finding the subject within it; some pools appear quite homogenous and lack a spot where the scent concentrates. But the biggest obstacle is that, except for the treeing hounds, dogs don't **expect** to find the object of their search activities overhead. You may see your dog stand with his nose in the air, tilting it this way and that, thoroughly puzzled. This is not the time to say,"Check it out," for the dog has already tried that; he has gone to the spot where the scent was strongest, but he can't tell where it is coming from. Go to your dog, look up at the subject--point him out if necessary, and praise the dog extravagantly. The more frustrated he has been, the greater reward is needed to bolster his motivation.

This is an instance where the dog can learn from a single experience all there is to know about the matter--essentially, people can be up on top of things. On his next try, he will look up at once when he reaches a maximum in a scent pool but finds nobody on the ground there.

The other cases are much harder to solve with air scent alone. The tiny cones rising from scent deposition in the subject's footprints may be stronger than the human body scent. Do not object if your dog goes to tracking or trailing. Dogs are practical; they use the best means available. If someone faults you for permitting your dog to abandon air scenting, tell him to set up his problem in an area where the ground scent is less potent or else allow you to enter it in the opposite direction from the subject. As your dog gains experience, you must not regiment his choice of media, because he can judge the most usable scent traces far better than you can.

In these cases, the dog may not alert at a distance, unless he gives a "track alert." He will probably go all the way to the subject and may be reluctant to return to you for the refind; for a buried subject, he may start digging or tearing off the cover with his teeth. The first time this happens, you should run to your dog and pour on the praise. When he has learned what to expect, however, encourage his refind by stepping back just out of sight and waiting for him to come get you--call him if you must. Continue this exercise intermittently until the refind is as good as the earlier ones, and even then an occasional review will do no harm.

Have your subject alternate the types of hiding places, and never, NEVER hide in the same, identical place twice in succession. The dog may conclude this place is natural people-habitat, just as the interface between a grain field and a woodlot is quail-habitat. Such a preconception will hamper a dog's search work and may cause him to bypass the actual hiding place because one he considers more likely looms up ahead.

THINGS TO THINK ABOUT

1. Does your dog quickly accept finding the subject in an unlikely spot? Does he detect the subject more readily when recumbent or when sitting upright on a branch (excluding movement, which of course draws the dog's attention)? Some dogs believe anyone capable of sitting or standing doesn't need to be rescued, so be sure your subjects assume a variety of postures in these sessions.

2. Can you tell by watching the dog how the scent is moving out of the hiding place and what quantity is present?

3. If another victim were hidden a few yards away, what is the probability that your dog would sense his presence? Try it.

4. In the Buried Victim search problem, must your dog run a finer search pattern (crisscross the area more frequently, with each pass close upon the preceding one, so that he goes within a few feet of every point in the area) to assure a 50% probability of detection? Why should this be true? How do temperature, humidity, wind, neighboring ground cover, and the material in which the victim is buried influence the size of the scent pool?

LESSON 7 - MOVING SUBJECT(S)

This exercise needs to be conducted in an area with enough cover or irregular terrain to prevent the subject from catching the dog's attention through his movement. Remember that dogs' eyes detect motion more readily than ours even at long distances. Instruct your subject to enter the agreed-upon section of the topographic map and wait until he hears you or the dog approaching. He should then commence to move down into an arroyo, around behind a row of bushes (**through** the bushes provides an audio clue, which you don't want) or into some other handy place of concealment.

When the dog approaches, the subject should stop and allow the dog to make sure of the find. Pretending to stumble and fall in the dog's path may stimulate the vacillating dog. On the first try, the subject should remain stationary during the recall and refind. On the second and subsequent tries, the subject may get up, drop something to mark the spot where the find occurred, and move off again so that when the dog returns with you, the refind will take place some distance away. Caution: intersperse this exercise with others, or the dog may become reluctant to do the recall for fear the subject will "get away" again.

If the dog seems confused or discouraged upon bringing you to the spot where he first found the subject, put him on lead and walk him around the spot until you see either an air or a track alert, then release him with praise: "Good dog! You've got it now! Go find!" Unless the wind is exactly right, the dog may correctly opt for tracking or trailing to pin the subject down. Allow him to use his best judgment.

When the dog is confident on a single moving subject, try two or three. Don't overdo it, though; you neither want to frustrate your dog nor to spoil his refind. Do this exercise just enough times to foster the dog's realization that a subject may be moving, or even running away. Devote at least 80% of your practice to the stationary case, because the unconscious or perfectly still human puts out very little scent and if the dog acquires too great an urgency in his search, he may run right over or past the more subtle scent traces.

THINGS TO THINK ABOUT

1. Observe the dog carefully as you approach the point where the subject ought to be, as shown by the marker. If he stands or sits still and tilts his head persistently in one direction, do you think he could be hearing rather than scenting the subject? Next time try an area with soft ground cover such as pine needles, where footsteps make no sound. Do not attempt to discourage the dog's using his ears; he should employ every

possible means of locating a lost person. (To learn how much farther away the dog can detect sounds than you can, ask on your radio for someone back in the parking area to count to ten, then honk the horn at 5-min. intervals during your return. Use your watch to measure how many intervals elapse between when your dog hears the horn and when you hear it?

2. Did the dog confidently show you the marker where he originally made the find, then immediately take off to relocate the subject? This is what you are aiming for. If the dog needs reassurance and additional commands to relocate, give them, but taper them off in subsequent tries. You want the dog to recognize what must be done-- to do his own thinking, rather than relying on you. Give low-key praise for the refind on the marker; omit the praise if you think it will distract the dog from completing the task.

3. With two or more moving victims, does the dog finish the refind on one before going after the other? Good. If he runs back and forth as if trying to look for both at once, put him on lead and insist he follow out one trace before attempting the second.

4. In a real search where you note from tracks in the mud that one subject is an adult and the other a child, which would you have the dog refind first? Why? If you think this depends on conditions, what would you consider other than weather?

LESSON 8 - TRAIL SEARCH; IGNORING FOLLOWERS

The trail search problem, as found in many certification tests or evaluations, consists of having the subject(s) hidden within 30 feet (or some other specified short distance) of a marked trail segment; the handler is constrained to stay on the trail while the dog ranges to either side, but the team may proceed to the end of the marked segment and return, making the find(s) on either pass. From the dog's viewpoint, this is like the searches you have already done except that you hold him to a tighter pattern, cover the same ground twice, and have two or more evaluators walking 50 or 100 yards behind, often chitchatting to each other. This last feature is the hardest part; it may distract **you** more than your dog!

If you wish to qualify for a team that has a trail search requirement, you will need to perfect this. Otherwise, give it a few tries to make sure your dog will not rebel at being put twice over the same ground or being held in to so close a pattern. It might someday be useful when searching in terrain so hazardous that the only place a foot-traveler can go is along the trail unless he sits or lies down beside it or falls off of it.

The trail search is usually set up by having the subject mark the start of the trail segment, walk the distance specified for the test (usually a quarter or half mile) as indicated by his pedometer, mark the end of the segment, and hide somewhere along the way back. This procedure may explain why so many dogs make their finds on the way back. Be sure to get two or three friends or classmates--without their dogs--to walk behind you, playing the role of evaluators. (If, in a real test, some evaluator starts to bring his dog along, OBJECT loud and clear. Your dog should not have to put up with competition when on trial.)

Give your dog his "Find 'em" command in the usual way, but be ready on the very first cast to turn him with your whistle or voice signal at or before twice the distance within which the subject is supposed to hide. For test-passing purposes, you want him to range a little beyond the hiding place to be sure of catching wind-borne scent, but not so far beyond that he would miss a tightly confined scent pool. On a real trail search, you would limit the range to how far the dog can travel safely; remember, he can't climb cliffs and rocks like a human, but he can detect scent borne up over them. (The scent will be not at the very edge of the cliff but some distance back from it--see Chapter IV.)

If you catch it right at the beginning, you will establish the short pattern in the dog's mind and after three or four swings won't have to worry about it further. You can help your dog get the picture by walking at a pace somewhat slower than normal yourself. This will give you the opportunity to fine-tune your control of the dog's pattern and also to observe more closely any tentative alert. (Remember, you are judged partially on how well you read your dog.)

When your dog alerts, no matter how indecisively, be sure to say, "Check it out." The dog could be wrong, or you could have imagined it, but an unproductive check-out won't cost you, whereas missing a vague alert on the first pass of the subject's hiding place (which the evaluators know in advance) could easily flunk you.

Your dog may not automatically recall if the subject is so close to the trail that you can't miss his find indication. My dogs point in a situation like this; others may stand with ears erect and look at their handler, or bark, or sit and stare. Go to the dog and praise him. Of course, if he does recall, pursue the refind as usual.

The presence of the evaluators should not bother the dog if you can keep him working well to the front. Do not allow him to loop back and "find" **them**. It will be easier not to let them make you nervous if you add a bit of stage-dressing: test the wind often even if you have a constant indication furnished by trail tape pinned to your thigh, look at your compass frequently, make notes, give lots of commands, direct your dog into likely cover despite his having scent-scanned it from a distance. This won't help or hinder the search (unless you get carried away and neglect to watch your dog) but it does impress the evaluators.

THINGS TO THINK ABOUT

1. Does the dog resist the tight pattern? Set up your next exercise in very thick cover, and have the subject fully hidden in a hollow or other scent trap. Hopefully, your dog will overrun the subject. Signal him back through the hollow in such a manner that he makes the find, so he understands that you may have a good reason for asking him to do something your way.

2. Does the dog look at you as if to say, "We've done that already," when you send him back the way you've just come? Repeat the command firmly. If he makes a find on the backswing, his reasoning will be as in the preceding question.

3. When the subject continues all the way to the end of the segment, then retraces his steps to hide, where will the predominant scent path be? Will scent tend to flow and pool in the open space above the trail, or will it filter into the surrounding cover? If the dog is directly on the trail at the point the subject left it, will he be more likely to notice the divergence than if he is 10 or 20 yards off at that point?

4. Does the dog's performance on this exercise, as compared with Lesson 7, support the belief that moving persons put out more scent than stationary ones?

LESSON 9 - CORRIDOR SEARCH

Your ability to control the dog's pattern and his forbearance toward other dogs may be severely challenged in the corridor search problem. Here, each dog/handler team is expected to cover a swath (usually 100 yards wide) parallel to that of another team on each side. Use open-enough country so that the handlers can see each other. Three teams are the minimum to practice this, and the exercise should be set up such that each gets a chance to be in the center, the most challenging position. Either run three short searches, or else proceed for fifteen or twenty minutes and then rotate corridors.

There should be a subject in each corridor, the same distance out from the starting point within 100 or 200 yards, so that each dog can make a find without leaving his assigned swath. The dog in the next corridor should catch scent from his own subject and make his alert by the time the one in the first corridor succeeds in his find. If you set up the first try at this exercise so it works out almost simultaneously, you will have much less trouble with the dogs' interfering with each other thereafter.

Some say dogs should not be so competitive as to try to "steal" a find. The competitive spirit varies with breed, individual temperament, and the relationship between the dogs involved. I have seen an old dog defer to a puppy, evidently trying to instruct it, and a half-grown pup defer to his adult role model, as if to learn by example. Dogs from the same pack may work well cooperatively without any special training.

However, if your dog cares enough to be diligent in a search despite all obstacles, he is bound to have a proprietary interest in the find. Dogs do tend to respect each other's territory, and we want in this exercise to teach them that their corridor is their territory. (Ignore the canine proprietary instinct at your own risk. If you think your dog is entitled to any find he can sense, don't be surprised when he gets mauled.)

All three handlers must understand that they are responsible for keeping their dogs within their respective corridors and attempt this exercise only when they are capable of doing so. Then procede as in any search problem, except that the handlers should try to maintain a straight line of advance. It is like the pole-probe line in avalanche rescue; when the line begins to straggle, the chances of a miss increase.

On subsequent attempts, the subjects can be progressively spread out so that the dog gets the idea, "Though I scent nobody in my corridor right now, there is bound to be someone farther on." No handler should permit his dog to go running over when another makes a find. After a successful refind, the dog should be praised highly and placed on leash, unless you have two sets of subjects in the corridors.

If your practice group is a large one and you have sufficient support personnel to use as subjects, this can be done with four, five, or more parallel corridors. In open terrain, such as a mesa top or expanse of prairie, the corridor search is extremely useful--especially when air flow patterns are such that scent is spotty, yet distant alerts suggest that the traces detected may have come from this locale.

THINGS TO THINK ABOUT

1. Do you have your dog under good enough control to keep him in his corridor without constant commands? If not, go back and work alone on some tight patterns in heavy brush before trying this again.

2. Is your dog distracted by another dog's find, or is he intent on doing his own job? You may have to remind him to stay with it the first few corridor searches--happily, he will make his own find quickly after his neighbor's, and next time it will be easier to keep his attention where it should be.

3. Does your dog cover his corridor well enough so you can state with 80% to 90% probability that he hasn't missed a subject? Repeat this exercise in an area with heavy cover. What adjustment must be made to the width of the corridors? After your search, compare notes with the other handlers; agree upon a realistic probability of detection (POD) for these circumstances .

4. If time and the number of teams and subjects available permit, try to ascertain the upper limit on the effective corridor width for moderately open country for these dogs. What is the POD? How rapidly can these dogs cover a corridor 1 mile long without unacceptable decrease in the POD? How long can dogs and handlers maintain this pace?

LESSON 10 - DISCRIMINATION

Some handlers argue against teaching air scent dogs to discriminate between one scent and another on the grounds that in a natural disaster, the number of victims present may be unknown to the searchers; and even if there is only one victim, a casual hiker the dog alerts on may be able to tell you of seeing him or signs of him. In the Los Alamos group, we have taught our dogs to discriminate for a particular person if given a scent object, but to alert on all people encountered if not given a scent object. When thus directed to discriminate, the dogs will indicate the presence of persons other than the one on whom they were scented but will not alert on them.

Granted, most (but not all) of these dogs were trained first for tracking or trailing. On a Tracking Dog Excellent problem, they will typically indicate the presence of the crosstracks but not take them--which prompted us to include discrimination in their air scent work. We have not found that doing so disrupted their basic air scenting in any way.

Set up a moderate-length search with three or more subjects, hidden within 100 feet of each other but not right together. One of the subjects should leave a fresh scent object in or by his car. (If the dogs in your group work well together, each can be scented on a different subject and all can do the exercise at once.) Pick up the scent object in a plastic bag, closing your fingers around it through the plastic and then pulling the edges up with the other hand so that you do not touch it (might as well get in practice for a real search). Hold the open top of the bag under the dog's nose and say, "Take scent...go find this one!"

Proceed as in previous searches. Watch the dog's alert; you may see two types, one for the person he was scented on and another for just anybody. Try to give your "Check it out" command with extra enthusiasm for the first type, which should be different--less tentative, perhaps--from what you have seen in earlier problems. If the dog runs up to the wrong subject, give your "Leave it" command (gently!), call him back to you, and re-scent him on the article in the bag, then repeat, "Go find this one!" The incorrect subject can help by ignoring the dog or telling him, "Off!" The correct subject should greet him joyously (just as in early training) when found.

On his first attempt, the dog may find discrimination hard to understand, but one redirection is often enough to give him the idea. You will know he grasps the point of the exercise when you see him approach an incorrect subject, sniff to make sure it is not the right one, and then continue in his pattern. After that, you may exchange a few words with the incorrect subjects after the dog indicates their presence, but keep the contact brief. Young dogs, with short attention spans, can easily forget what their objective is if their efforts are interrupted for any considerable time. Even wtih older dogs, you may undo what you have accomplished if you treat the indication as a find. Save your rewards for the discovery of the correct subject.

Dogs that have tracked or trailed will pick this up in one or two sessions. Those started on air scent may not even understand how to take scent on their first try, until they see how they are expected to use it. Be patient, be quietly firm. If a mistake is made, calmly say, "Leave it" and present the article again. All dogs can discriminate, and one that does is much more useful on a real search through woods full of hunters and campers. Don't be one who makes the co-ordinator call in all the other teams so that your dog can work without interference.

THINGS TO THINK ABOUT

1. Does your dog take scent readily? If he doesn't seem to understand what you want of him, walk him a few steps along the path the subject must have taken (a good reason for having him leave the scent article on the driver's seat of his car). If you see a footprint or portion of one where the trail goes onto soft ground, point to the print and urge the dog to compare its scent with the article scent. Then repeat the command "Go find this one."

2. Does your dog attempt to track? Let him! Often the most effective strategy is to track the subject into the general neighborhood of his hiding place, then go to the air when scent pools or other obstacles cause loss of track. Since most dogs greatly prefer air scent when they can detect enough to work with, you don't need to fear he will track too much. But if he's tracking more than you like, run ahead of him and shout eagerly, "Go find that one!" You probably can run faster than he can track. Give your signal to range out. When pushed for speed, he will tend to go to the air.

3. How does your dog alert on the right person? On an incorrect one? Is the latter so different that you know at once it is merely an indication?

4. Does your dog not seem to understand discriminating? Next time, instruct your subject to leave, just outside his hiding place, the mate to the glove or sock left in his car as a scent object. Should the dog miss it, call it to his attention, saying, "Look here! Take scent." Let the dog compare it with the one in the bag. He will naturally then air scent his way to the nearby hiding place. Praise him--immediately! Do not wait for a refind until he does this with assurance. Only then should you require a recall and refind.

5. Does your dog ignore all incorrect persons entirely? Repeat the exercise, watching carefully for the slightest indication. It is probably there, although it may not be obvious. Praise the dog, go to the incorrect person and chat a moment before sending the dog on. This simulates the situation where a casual hiker may have seen the victim and can tell you something helpful ("He was trying to climb down the waterfall two hours ago.")

EVIDENCE SEARCH

LESSON PLAN

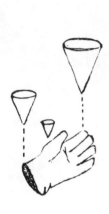

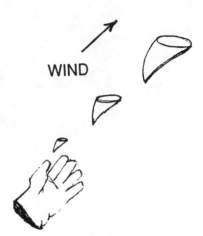

Scent cones in still air.   *Scent cones in wind.*

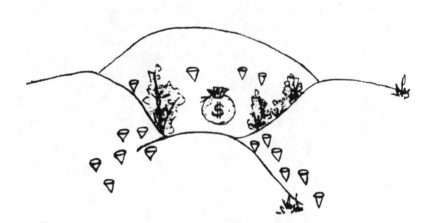

*Scent pool around article,
showing leakage.*

EVIDENCE SEARCH LESSON PLAN

Objectives. The dog that has learned to find articles while completing the Tracking and Trailing Lesson Plan is easily taught to find only articles bearing a particular person's scent. In case you need to leave the article where it was found for use as evidence, you will want the dog to indicate it without touching it and to signal you that he has found what you were searching for--or do a refind (bring you to it) rather than picking it up and bringing it to you.

In real searches, the evidence may not be right on the track as in AKC work. A lost person may throw a beer can into a nearby hole as he wanders. The bank robber may toss the bag of money Into a thicket if he thinks pursuers are hot on his trail, with the intention of recovering it later. You can train your dog to detect these articles from the scent pool they generate and find them although they are several dozen yards off the track. You can teach the dog to find them even if dirt has been piled on top of them or snow has drifted over them.

You might want your dog to find an object by its own odor rather than that of a person who has handled it--a gun, a knife, an ax, a can of gasoline. After you have taught this, you can ask the dog to search for any object or substance just by scenting him on a similar one. My old Duke once directed a Forest Service officer to a whole string of illegal steel traps in this manner. Dogs have been used to detect smoke, gas leaks, bombs, drugs, etc. After finding an illegal substance (such as evidence of arson), dogs can lead a handler to the hiding place of the person who put it there.

Evidence search is particularly useful in everyday life. When you drop your car key, scent the dog on your house key to make the find. Scent him on the purse or pocket in which you were carrying your lost billfold. This lesson plan is very practical for the average person. It offers a rich return on the few weeks required to learn the skill.

Equipment required. Your dog should have a plain leather or fabric collar and a non-restrictive harness. You may want a short (2-6 foot) leather lead or one of the retractable leads that the dog has not learned to associate with tracking.

In this lesson plan, we will gradually wean the dog from using a human ground track. Because your dog has learned in his prior training that your scent is generally irrelevant, you will probably want to serve as your own tracklayer after completing Lesson 3.

You will need several examples of whatever it is you want the dog to search for on any particular day. (As you begin to train, the dog will learn faster if you have him seek one distinctive odor per session. Save the finding of two or more substances simultaneously for an advanced exercise.) Miscellaneous items are fine for the beginning lessons, and specific objects will be listed for later ones, but you should apply the same principles to any other classes of articles that you may need to locate.

Commands. Because evidence search has some important differences from your previous scent work, you must decide before you begin on a new command for this activity. If you have established a verbal "Track it" command to start the dog along a ground scent trail and a verbal "Go find" command to initiate air scenting, you might want to try a "Find this" or "Where's another one?" command for evidence search.

Many dogs really can learn a word for a particular class of object (for example, "Find gun," or "Find money") despite some behaviorists' opinion. It is certainly easier to say, "Find gun," for practical purposes, than it is to have to go and get one to scent the dog if firearms are not part of your working uniform. You teach the word by using it while you are scenting the dog on one object of the class (say, "Take scent. Gun," as you point to the item; then give the "Find gun" command to start the dog's search). After you are sure the dog knows the word, you can omit the "Take scent" portion of the starting procedure. Dogs vary considerably in their ability to learn large numbers of words; therefore, you risk less frustration by letting a single word represent an entire class than by using an individual word for each object: teach "gun" rather than "rifle + pistol + holster + ammo + ..."

As with most canine abilities, the size of your dog's potential vocabulary is strongly dependent on how large you believe it is. If you are convinced a dog can only learn a dozen or so commands, then you will be more successful if you limit yourself to the verbal "Find this" direction, preceded by scenting the dog on an object similar to the one you want him to find.

LESSON 1 - FINDING EVIDENCE BUT NOT DISTURBING IT

Preparation: Ask your tracklayer for a five-leg track about 250 paces long with scent articles at the start, the finish, and two per leg in between. . Lay the first track in a level, isolated place; later ones, on difficult terrain or heavily used ground. Ask the tracklayer to draw a clear map and mark the approximate positions of the articles. Age the track 4 to 24 hours.

Running the track. Look over the map. Fix firmly in your mind the locations of the articles so that you can keep your entire attention on the dog: "...at the start, by the big rock midway in leg 1, at the base of the tree near turn 2, in the hollow near the end of leg 3...total articles, 9."

Put on the harness and bring your dog to the start on lead. Point to the article while you move the snap to the D-ring, saying, "Take scent--careful!" **Don't pick it up or let the dog touch it.** Start the dog with a command that emphasizes the article (see p. 92 for various possibilities).

Maintain enough tension on the lead to slow the dog down so that he works step by step, rather than trailing. Watch for the alert as he approaches each article's location. Remember that an object foreign to the area acts as a point source and gives off a cone-shaped scent cloud (fanning out downwind if the breeze is brisk, rising almost vertically in the absence of wind). An article in a hollow or protected spot will give rise to a sizeable scent pool on a well-aged track. The dog will indicate the edge of a pool in some way--his head may snap up, he may stop dead in his tracks, he may bark or growl.

Praise his alert, no matter how subtle; this will encourage him to give a stronger alert the next time. Tell him, "Good boy, check it out," or whatever similar command you have been using. Let out enough lead so he can go almost to the article. Careful! You want to stop him before he can pick it up, but so smoothly that he does not feel he is being corrected.

Out of frustration at not being able to reach the article, the dog will undoubtedly give some sign: a bark, a whine, pawing at the ground. If you overdid your restraint, he may sit or lie down; some handlers deliberately teach their dogs this signal. Others evoke a bark by saying, "Speak." In searching for dangerous articles or for disaster victims, the bark is the best find indication; a dog flopping down on a pile of rubble could cause it to cave in and suffocate the victim. A bark is much safer. Encourage a sharp single or double "arf." A frenzy of barking is undesirable.

At the dog's signal, praise him verbally and approach with caution: let the dog know you appreciate his advising you to be careful. Go hand over hand along the lead, maintaining enough tension to keep the dog from lunging at the article and grabbing it. When you reach the article, praise and treat the dog with one hand while you acknowledge the article and simulate marking its location with the other. **Don't** pick it up. You can thrust a survey flag into the ground a foot or so from it, or set a trio of flags around it as you would in a real situation, or just scratch a circle around it in the earth.

Now lead the dog carefully around the article, put him back on the trail, and say, "Where's another one?" or give a similar command. It doesn't hurt to overact, especially if your dog has been eagerly bringing you articles or was force-broken to retrieve. Pretend you, yourself, are scared of touching the thing. A set mousetrap on the article, or an overinflated balloon that will burst with a loud pop, may be needed to impress a really determined dog.

When the dog has indicated the last article and you have reacted to it, give your "That's all" or "At ease" signal and take the dog past the article for his praise and/or treats. Make these generous; a dog finds it much harder fo to overcome his retrieving instinct than to grab up what he considers prey.

THINGS TO THINK ABOUT

1. What sign did your dog give on detecting the edge of an article's scent pool? Was the indication stronger for subsequent articles?

2. What sign did the dog give that the article was right there, just out of his reach, the first time? Subsequent times?

3. Do you think you overdid the restraint? If your dog seems confused or put off by frustration, do some plain tracking problems. Then try this again, starting the restraint farther from the article and applying it gradually.

4. Did the addition of obstacles to the scenting process distract the dog? Run some tracks without obstacles, then add obstacles gradually.

LESSON 2 - EVIDENCE OFF THE TRACK

Preparation. The tracklayer should proceed as in Lesson 1 except that an article on each leg should be thrown off the track in the windward direction, a foot or so at first, progressing up to several feet. Plan to run the track after it has aged about half an hour. Near sundown or sunup when the wind direction usually changes, the articles should be thrown in the direction from which the wind will probably be coming when the track is run.

Wind strength must also be considered. In a light breeze or still air, limit the distance the article is thrown to 3 or 4 feet. In a steady, moderate-to-strong wind, an article may be thrown as far as the tracklayer can manage (use heavy, compact articles). In a gusty, undependable wind, keep the distance short. With experience, most dogs can detect articles many paces off the track, but allow them to build up this skill gradually.

Running the track. As in the previous lesson, it will help to essentially memorize the map before starting. The dog's alert on a distant article may differ from that on an article right in front of his nose, where its scent is mingled with the tracklayer's body scent. Be watchful so you don't miss it.

When you see an alert, give your "Check it out" command. Allow the dog enough lead to seek actively, but not so much that he can grab the article. Note the dog's signal when he achieves a firm location of the article. Again, mark its presence, but don't pick it up. Praise the dog as you walk him back to the track, then command, "Find more" or "Find another." As the dog starts off again, restrain any tendency to backtrack towards the starting point. The word "another" or "more" should convey that you want him to proceed from where he left off.

At the last article, follow your praise with the "That's all" command or signal. Then you can tell him, "Find the car." His heading off crosscountry directly towards the parking area is preferable to taking you back step by step the way you came--it saves time and effort on a U-shaped course.

THINGS TO THINK ABOUT

1. Did you catch the dog's alert on the edge of the scent pool? Making careful note of where these alerts occur with respect to the object each time will build up your knowledge of what his detection limit may be under various conditions.

2. How did your dog follow up on his alert? You will see some comb the grass with their noses, snuffling loudly and moving in ever- increasing arcs. Others will stand with nose up testing the airflow, then work side to side with decreasing swings as they near the apex of the scent cone. Still others

will use either ground scent or air scent depending on their judgment of the conditions, or alternate between the two if the location of the object requires much time. No single way is right. With experience, the dog will know what is most effective for him.

3. Are you learning to read the dog's signal for an evidence find? Is the dog progressively accepting the need to leave evidence undisturbed?

4. Do you see any slackening of the dog's interest in articles now that he is not allowed to pick them up? Guard against this by boosting your praise of the finds. One sure sign of flagging motivation is a tendency for the dog to miss or cease to indicate articles.

5. Does the dog show curiosity and/or satisfaction when you put in the marker flags around the object? Good. This demonstrates his recognition that he has done the job despite not getting the article in his mouth.

6. When the dog appears to have mastered this problem, try having the articles placed downwind of the track (limit the distance to 3 or 4 feet the first time). Can the dog still find the articles? How does he do it? If time permits, set up some problems to test the limit of detectability for articles downwind. Such knowledge could avoid your leaving a hole in your coverage and overestimating your probability of detection.

LESSON 3 - THE HIDDEN ARTICLE

Preparation. In this sequence, the tracks should be relatively short with the articles very close together. Be sure not to cut the track age to under half an hour or you give scent pools a chance to form. Ask the tracklayer to alternate in placing the articles upwind and downwind of the scent path. If the second article is in a hollow 4 feet to the right, the third might be hung on a bush 6 feet to the left (scent will tend to be confined by the hollow, and to spread down and out from the above-ground location unless the airflow is straight up--see Chapter IV).

The second week, if your dog is doing well, add challenge by first partially, and then completely, burying the low articles, and placing the high ones in a treetop or up on a large boulder that the dog cannot climb. If that goes well, get two tracklayers and have the first lay out about half the track in a loop that swings back to a road or path by which the second can meet him and take over. Have the second tracklayer place an article only a few paces beyond where he starts work the first time. The reason for this is to finish shifting the dog's focus from the person who placed the articles to the articles themselves. Sometimes you will want to find a thing that has been transferred from one person to another; other times you will want to find things with no track at all between them, such as leaks in a gas line.

There are two ways of de-emphasizing human scent on the articles. One is to minimize it--use new items packaged in plastic and open the package only to drop the objects out, not touching them at all. The other is to hide the tracklayer's scent amongst many other human scents--have everyone at the site handle all the articles before the tracklayers start out.

Running the track. Do not be surprised if the dog is somewhat puzzled by having to hunt down or up for the articles. Allow him all the time he needs after his alert to comb the area. Only if he gets so frustrated that his efforts become wild and inefficient should you point out the article; he will remember much better if he makes the find himself.

Especially with the overhead article and the fully buried one, you may see the dog do a double-take as if a light suddenly dawns. He will then act very pleased with himself, and you should run to him with lots of praise, overlooking a too-exuberant find signal. The dog has made a major breakthrough. Next time he faces the same problem, he'll know how to handle it, and you can go back to the cautious approach.

This reaction generally means the dog has made the shift from visual recognition of the article's presence to knowing its location from its scent alone. You no longer have to produce it for him to reassure him that he has really made a find. You can just mark the spot and proceed to your next training exercise..

THINGS TO THINK ABOUT

1. Is there any difference in the dog's ability to find things up high as opposed to down low? Which seems easier? (This will differ from dog to dog.)

2. Does the dog's find signal seem tentative at first when the articles are completely out of sight? You may need to reveal the article and show it to the dog to assure him he has been successful before you replace it and mark the spot. After one or two times, your marking action should be all he needs.

3. How far off the track does the dog locate an article hidden below the usual scent level, as compared with one lying in the open on flat ground? An article placed above ground level? What are the relative detection limits in various conditions?

4. When you change tracklayers, does the dog seem confused? Does his uncertainty dissolve when he hits the edge of the scent pool from the next article? (It should. If not, let the second tracklayer's initial article be right at the changeover point on your next try.) Assuming that your practice group is large enough, you can have a different person lay each short leg of a zigzag course whose overall pattern parallels an access path.

5. As you continue after the change, do you see signs that the dog is paying less attention to the ground track and is actually beginning to air scent from article-pool to article-pool? For evidence search, this is good and should not be discouraged.

LESSON 4 - FINDING A PARTICULAR SCENT FROM A SOLID SUBSTANCE

Preparation. Get together a collection of spent cartridges from a field handler's or referee's starting pistol, and a pistol itself that has been fired recently. (Similar objects can be used, but this is an easy and cheap way to do it.) The intent is to teach your dog to look for the articles by their gunpowder smell, which is quite distinctive and strong enough that you can actually smell it yourself if conditions are favorable.

The track should be short and the objects close together on the first try; then it should be lengthened in subsequent attempts. Each drop should consist of two or three spent blanks in a little mesh bag, up to the last one which is the gun itself. The drops should be 3 or 4 feet off the track to one side or the other. If you make up the bags of blanks and put them and the gun in a plastic bag so that the tracklayer can open the top and dump the articles one at a time without actually touching them, they will have very little of his scent on them and the dog will be free to concentrate on the article scent. It is not possible for a person to carry objects any distance, even in a plastic bag, without getting **some** scent on them; but with this procedure, the tracklayer's scent is much fainter than your scent, which your dog has by now learned to largely ignore.

Try to age this track 4 hours or more if there is little wind. The time can be shorter when conditions are such as to dissipate the tracklayer's air scent path faster. The ground scent will still be there, but if the tracklayer dumps the bags as far off his path as he can reach, the ground scent will not be much of a distraction.

Running the track. Make a big production out of having the dog take scent on the first object. We have never before asked him to hunt strictly for a particular kind of thing, and we have to call special attention to it.

If your articles are close enough together and far enough off the track, and the age is sufficient, the scent pools from the drops should almost overlap. Do not try to make the dog track; you want him to look for the next pool, and the next. After all this practice, he should take your word for it that a scent pool will occur shortly. After a few of these problems, he will accept an extended separation as long as he hasn't heard your "That's all" command--but you should work up to it gradually.

Make the dog feel like a hero when he finds the gun. However, you must do so without letting him disturb it. If you ever come across a loaded gun, you don't want your dog to touch it for safety reasons. Just think how embarrasing it would be to end your search in the hospital because your dog picked up the evidence and accidentally discharged it in your direction. Again, try to stimulate the dog's recognition that guns are dangerous by acting as if you yourself are afraid of it.

THINGS TO THINK ABOUT

1. Did the dog readily take scent on the first collection of spent cartridges, or did he seem to be looking for a strong human scent (other than yours)? If the latter, did the dog take scent on the cartridges the second time you exposed him to this problem?

2. When he came upon the scent pool from the next collection of cartridges, did the dog appear to understand what you wanted? Although most dogs will, those that have completed the Air Scent Lesson Plan will probably grasp it more quickly than others. If the dog still hasn't caught on by the end of the first session, have your tracklayer make the drops extremely close together for the next try.

3. Are the dog's alert and find signals noticeably different from what you have observed in previous exercises?

4. Did the dog show extra enthusiasm for the last article, the gun? Good! Reinforce with extra praise.

5. On the second and third tries, did the dog start acting as if the gun was the object of the search and the small bags of cartridges were merely its "tracks"? This is very desirable. When this behavior is observed, the dog is ready to proceed with a new lesson.

LESSON 5 - SEARCHING FOR A LIQUID OR GASEOUS SUBSTANCE

Preparation. As in Lesson 4, you should make ready the "articles" yourself so that the tracklayer's scent will not be a large component of their characteristic odor. Use something porous like a piece of terry cloth or a sponge that can be saturated in a volatile liquid. .Tie or fasten this to a stone or fishing weight--something heavy--so it can be thrown and will stay where it falls until found. Put these objects in a plastic bag.

The substance can be gasoline, lamp fuel, motor oil, vinegar, cheap perfume, alcohol--preferably one that doesn't evaporate so fast that you have to run the track before the tracklayer's scent has dissipated. At least on the early attempts, don't use beer. Most areas are so littered with old beer cans lying around that there's too great a chance of unwanted distraction. Advise the tracklayer to handle the objects with care; most of the effective substances for this are quite flammable or even explosive.

As with the gunpowder problem, the track should be relatively short, and on the initial try, the distance between drops should be small. The last object should be an empty can or bottle that held the substance, or if a fuel, a lamp or camp stove in which it has been burned. We want the dog to see a "track...track...track...major find" effect.

Running the track. Scent the dog on the first object and give your "Find another" command. After the gunpowder series, the dog should air scent his way to the pool from the second object with little or no hesitation.

Be watchful from the time you see the alert until the find. Depending on what volatile substance you are using, you may have to exert much more control to keep your dog from grabbing the object. Antifreeze, for example, has an odor that is strongly attractive to dogs, and many are poisoned every year by ingesting it. If your dog is still resisting your "Danger--don't touch" command by the end of the first session, treat the objects with a dog repellent. But don't do this unless absolutely necessary; the dog should leave the object alone because of your command, not because it smells bad. Besides, some dogs don't respond to repellents.

If your dog wants to work rapidly from pool to pool, minimize the time you spend marking the finds. Thrust in a single flag beside each object, and only use three or four flags around the final one. Do maintain plenty of praise.

THINGS TO THINK ABOUT

1. Does the dog quickly grasp what you want in this problem? If so, have the tracklayer extend the distance between drops on the second try. (A volatile substance makes a large scent pool quickly, and the dog can

detect it quite far off.) How does relative humidity affect the detection distance?

2. Does the dog try to rush in on the object? Redouble your restraint, and your "Danger" indication.

3. Does the dog alert but not zero in to find? He is trying to bypass the object. Increase your lead tension, or even back up until he is where he alerted and then give your "Check it out" command. Don't permit the dog to skip an article.

4. Is the dog repelled by the objects? If so, he may ignore them, or he may try to attack and destroy them. Neither of these reactions can be tolerated. Treat the first as if he were skipping objects from boredom or impatience, the second as if he were **too** attracted to them. The dog's job is to find the objects, not to express an opinion about them. He should leave the reacting to you.

5. Do you still see indications that the dog is trying to track rather than air scent? Lay one trail with minimal ground scent by having someone drive a truck with a camper shell over a field while you sit in the back, throwing the objects out at intervals. If the cab is tightly closed, this should result in a trail with very little human scent, and that mostly yours, which the dog has learned to ignore. Do this only once or twice, or your dog will start tracking the truck. (Of course, you can use this exercise to teach him to track motor vehicles if you wish).

6. Do you see indications of the dog's scent ability being saturated by these volatile substances? If so, how soon does this effect appear?

LESSON 6 - FINDING EDGED WEAPONS, METALLIC ARTICLES

Preparation. Use knives, scissors, files, a small ax. If the first has been recently sharpened, that may help. The metal objects should be closer together than the volatile drops were, because they will generate smaller scent pools. Increasing the age of the "track" will allow the dog to detect the objects at greater distances.

With the exception of fence wire, worked metal is generally anomalous in wilderness areas and therefore quite noticeable. If the first and second tries at this go exceedingly well, you may wish to make the problem more challenging by shifting to a locale such as an automobile graveyard or dump where metallic smells are very common. This task is not too hard for the dog; public school security officers use dogs to detect edged weapons inside student lockers that are composed of metal.

Running the problem. Give the dog plenty of time as he takes scent on the first object. The metallic scent is more subtle than the article scents we worked on in the previous lessons.

A slower pace than on the volatiles may be more productive. If the dog does not adopt a careful, deliberate way of working on his own, you can slow him down with lead tension. After he realizes you have prevented his overrunning an article by stopping or backing up, he will probably see that a more cautious approach works better.

If the dog alerts on and finds a metal object that was not planted for him, treat it as if it was a regular, scheduled find. Remember that you have asked him to look for metal, not just metal bearing fresh human scent, and you must not penalize him for doing what he was told.

Redouble the praise and reward for this. It is a harder task, and not nearly so much fun.

THINGS TO THINK ABOUT

1. What is the dog's detection distance for metallic objects? Is this affected more or less by humidity and wind conditions than the detection distance for volatile substances?

2. Are you maintaining the dog's motivation?

3. Does the dog have trouble recognizing a distinctive metallic scent on the first try? For the next attempt, rub the articles with a whetstone or a file before packaging them up for the tracklayer; the roughened, freshly-exposed surface will put out more of its characteristic scent. Then try again with articles not recently sharpened.

4. Add one or two aluminum objects. Are the dog's reactions to these the same as to steel? Sniff both a steel and an aluminum object, with your eyes closed. Do they smell different? Will your dog find aluminum if scented on steel? Try it.

5. Substitute kitchen utensils for some of the weapons or tools. Does the dog consider these the same class of object--or does he find only whichever he was scented on? (Some dogs categorize more broadly than others. You need to know what to expect of yours.)

6. Do one session using only garden tools. Let the first be a hoe, a shovel, or something else that has dug in the earth. Will the dog discriminate for gardening objects? (You can check this by placing one or two articles from your auto tool box along the way, but no matter what the dog does, he should be praised--this is just for you to find out what kind of distinctions he makes in classifying objects.)

7. Let the dog make one or more tries at this off-lead. Does he maintain a sensible working pace? Does he refrain from disturbing the evidence as he makes the find? If both answers are affirmative, you can work your future evidence searches off-lead.

LESSON 7 - FINDING MONEY OR JEWELS, IDENTIFYING TRACKLAYER

Preparation. For the first try, use an assortment of coins in a cloth bag or purse; for the second, mix coins and paper money; for the third, use costume jewelry. By this time, your dog should be ready to find whatever object you scent him on, as long as there is something distinctive about its scent. On subsequent tries, alternate these three kinds of articles, and sometimes use a paper bag with a stone inside to give weight (unless the ground is wet enough to soften paper). You should be so good by now that you don't need a map, so let your only prior knowledge be the total number of objects that are out there to be found.

As these items will always have human scent on them, make no attempt to keep them unscented while they are being planted; you may want several people to handle them before starting to assure that they have many different scents. We also want them at varying distances from the track, and occasionally we want more than one article in a drop. When the dog is detecting all three types of item well, try a variation. Work with friends to set up a problem where **you** do not know who the tracklayer is and, rather than putting out all the articles, have this person keep the last one in a pocket and return to mingle with the group in the parking area. The dog's task will be to find the last article and thereby identify the tracklayer.

Running the track. Let the dog take scent as in the other substance problems and choose his own method of working. If he uses the ground track, do not attempt to discourage this, but do not try to keep him from air scenting, either.

Be sure not to rush the dog when he is checking it out. His alert may have been on a double article and if you hurry him, he will find only one of the two present in that particular scent pool.

Work the first one or two of these on lead, then try one off lead. If the dog gets too far ahead, use your "Wait up" verbal command.

On the final problem, the dog will be leading you back to the parking area after you have found one less than the total number of articles you know were originally planted. Watch the dog carefully as he approaches the group; be ready to run up and restrain any too-aggressive approach to the tracklayer. The dog's identification should be of the "Danger--take care" type.

THINGS TO THINK ABOUT

1. Does the dog lock onto the coins and jewelry readily enough from his recent practice with the metallic problem, but fail to see why anyone should worry about silly green strips of paper? Do another problem or two in which currency and coins are both planted together.

2. Would the dog find a money/jewelry bag that was thrown into the bushes when the thief realized you were catching up with him? Can he find it if it is dropped in a hole and covered with a stone?

3. Does the dog use tracking and air scent skills, depending on which is more appropriate for the conditions, to make the find the quickest, surest way?

4. Does the dog readily identify the tracklayer and point out the pocket in which he has concealed the last object?

5. Have the tracklayer return to the group, but, while you are out on the trail, pass the object to another person in the group and have that person put it in a pocket. Does the dog go to the tracklayer, and only then go to the second person to point out the pocket, or does he go directly to the person who now has it? (In the first case, your dog was probably tracking the tracklayer; in the second, he was probably air scenting for the object. However, he **could** have used air scent to show where the object previously was as well as where it is now, because the pocket will retain and emit some of the object's scent even when the object has been removed.)

DISASTER SEARCH AND AGILITY

LESSON PLAN

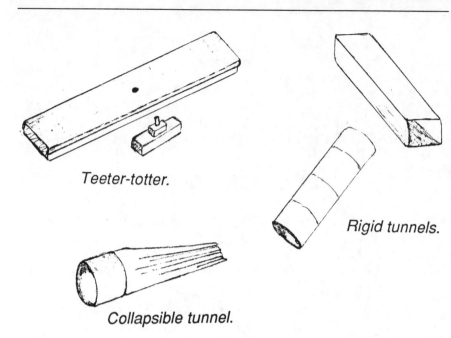

Teeter-totter.

Rigid tunnels.

Collapsible tunnel.

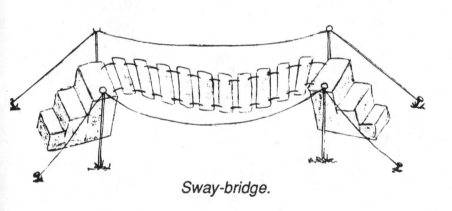

Sway-bridge.

Equipment for agility training.

LESSON PLAN FOR DISASTER SEARCH AND AGILITY

Objectives. In any disaster, the search dog faces two types of problem. First, the site is difficult, dangerous, and possibly frightening to move around in, whether it is a small area (collapsed building, wrecked train) or a quite extensive one (flood, tornado, major earthquake). Second, the site is often permeated by impediments to scenting (spilled motor fuel, chemicals, smoke fumes, clouds of dust, decaying water-logged debris). This lesson plan prepares the dog and handler for both.

Disaster dogs usually work off-lead because of the obstacles they must traverse. Dogs can go where no human could venture safely. But they must be taught to climb, crawl into restricted spaces, move carefully on unstable footing, choose a safe path through smoking embers or broken glass. To train, we use teeter-boards, swaying bridges, tunnels, and other items associated with Agility competition, but there the resemblance stops. Speed and abject obedience are the last things we want. The disaster dog must choose a safe path where he can go, judge where he cannot go without unacceptable risk, and simultaneously conduct an effective search.

It has been demonstrated that certain odors will mask human scent or reduce the dog's ability to detect it by several orders of magnitude. Nonetheless, we hear of dogs (especially Bloodhounds) following an old trail through a large machine shop or a fume-filled superhighway interchange. Weimaraner handlers of my personal acquaintance found their dogs could detect where numerous flood victims lay buried despite the stench of decaying debris in Colorado's Big Thompson Canyon in 1977. Handlers who smoke insist their cigarettes don't interfere with **their** dogs' noses because "they are used to it." We therefore train in the presence of interfering odors to enhance the dogs' ability to screen out strong background scents and detect the particular one they are looking for. We help the handler gauge the degree of interference and the adjustments they must make in reading the dog when such substances are present.

These dogs generally work by air scenting, because major disasters often wipe out ground trails or dump victims into the middle of the search area without giving them a chance to leave a trail. The lessons do give some practice finding clues and articles as well as people, however.

Equipment needed. The dog wears a plain leather or fabric collar that won't catch on things. A 6-foot obedience lead or a retractable lead is used in the beginning agility practice, together with a throw-toy, a retrieving object, or food treats. Representative obstacles and interfering substances are detailed in each exercise.

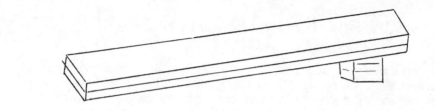

Lumber (simulates log)

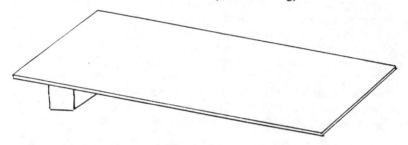

Plywood (used as ramp)

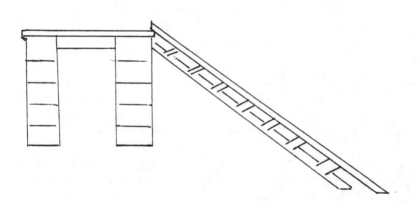

Ladder and platform (plywood on cement blocks).

Commonly available items usable as agility training equipment.

LESSON 1 - INTRODUCTION TO AGILITY

Preparation. Lay out a simple obstacle course. Use whatever is at hand on your practice grounds, such as a low wall that a dog can walk along while the handler walks on the ground beside it, a cardboard box or 55-gal. drum with the ends cut out for a tunnel, a teeter-board with the bare wood side up propped on two solid blocks (don't let it teeter yet!), a piece of metal siding laid flat on the ground, a ladder laid flat on the ground, a log or half-hoop that the dog must crawl under.

The obstacles should be placed 20 paces or more apart so that the dog can recover his confidence before facing the next one. In a class situation, this spacing permits some members to work at each obstacle unhampered by those on either side. A few obstacles will suffice, but always include some of each type (elevated, closed in/submerged, doubtful footing).

Working procedure. Bring the dog, on lead, to the first obstacle. Let him sniff it. Back off, approach the obstacle again, then take the dog over/through/under it while you walk alongside, dropping the lead as necessary. If the dog crosses the obstacle confidently beside you, take the third step: throw or place a retrieve article on the other side and send the dog for it (he should traverse the obstacle both going and returning). Otherwise, repeat the second step, rest and reassure the dog, then try again until he is confident; three tries without a break.

The tunnel may require that you heel the dog part way through the entrance, drop the lead, run quickly to the far end, call, and grab the lead as the dog emerges--or even throw a toy/treat ahead as you start him in. You may need to have someone to hold the dog while you run to the far end of the tunnel, and then release him when you call.

The wall or elevated board may require a short lead and much verbal reassurance on the first try to keep the dog from jumping down. You may have to walk on the flat sheet metal yourself to convince the dog it's safe, then walk beside it while he walks on it the next time. With all obstacles, take a break for rest and reassurance after three tries.

For the ladder or interrupted footing, another person the dog trusts can handle the lead while you actually place his feet until he gets the idea. Do it slowly, one foot at a time; and remember that the dog can't see his back feet so he has to feel for the next step-- move his foot in the empty space between and then onto the step just as he will have to do himself. If your dog is small, you can set him down on the middle of the obstacle so that he must make an effort to get off of it. Be ready to calm and restrain him from doing so in a single wild jump; you're trying to teach him that panic is self-defeating, but cautious persistence will get him where he wants to go.

Quiet heeling over the obstacles may be as far as you get during the first session. That's all right, but do try to make it that far. Then your second session will be off to a good start. Don't make more of the obstacles than the dog does, though; if you approach them in a matter-of-fact way, he may cross them without hesitation the very first time. Don't assume the next obstacle will be a problem just because the last one was--some dogs are hesitant about tunnels but go over bridges 12 feet off the ground without a second look; others are just the opposite.

Toward the end of this week, if all is going well, have someone hold your dog (or put him on a "stay") while you go to the end of the course and call. If your dog comes readily to you over all the obstacles, try it again, hiding out of sight. Then have the other person hide at the end of the course, and send the dog to find him. Use a new find command, such as "Hunt--careful now.".

THINGS TO THINK ABOUT

1. Which type of obstacle is hardest for the dog? Which is easiest? Do none of them present a problem? Good. Go on to the next lesson.

2. Does your being out of sight appear to bother the dog? Give him extra practice on the tunnel.

3. After a few times over, does the dog go through the whole course without particularly thinking about it? Good, but you want him to remain cautious. Put the teeter-board higher above the ground, set some of the ladder steps farther apart (or remove one or two), extend the tunnel.

4. Does the dog attempt to skip one or more obstacles? Put toys or treats on them for him to pick up on his way (first on-lead, then off.).

5. Will your dog go through the whole course and make a find at the end? If not, spend another week on this lesson.

LESSON 2 - ADVANCED AGILITY

Preparation. Choose a place where your course can end at some natural feature the dog may find threatening: a hollow under rocks, a small cave, an overhanging bank, a large culvert. Towards evening, the entrance to a deserted building or a small shed will do. If no such location is available, use a large cardboard box or 55-gal. drum. Supply a tarp or piece of plywood to cover the entrance so that the dog cannot get in readily.

Set up an obstacle course as in Lesson 1, ending at the hiding place. Reduce the space between obstacles (unless required for class work); by now, your dog should not need recovery time, and disaster searches often take place in a limited area with many hazards concentrated in one spot.

Increase the degree of difficulty in every obstacle. Make the tunnel smaller and longer, add another section to form a right-angle turn. Set the elevated board waist-high, with a ramp at each end (a dog can injure himself jumping down, even the height of his withers). Add a collapsible tunnel.

Remove the end-blocks from the teeter-board so the dog needs to go up it to the center, shift his weight so the far end goes down, then descend the other side. Let the barrier that the dog has to crawl under be **really** low, down in a hollow if possible, and drape the opening with a towel that the dog must push aside. Lay a piece of plywood over a log so that the whole slab acts as a teeter-board. Set the ladder on a shallow incline leading up to a platform. Five or six obstacles are enough for any one course; use others on subsequent courses so that the dog doesn't know what to expect next.

Working the course. Attempt each obstacle except the last separately, using the three steps listed in Lesson 1. Now take the dog on lead through the course except for the last obstacle. If that goes well, have someone hide under or behind the obstacle. Say "Hunt--careful" or whatever disaster-search command you have chosen, and let the dog precede you through the course, watching him intently.

When you see the alert, tell the dog, "Check it out--careful now!" (or "danger" or whatever is your caution word). Allow him to approach the hidden subject but not go all the way, restraining him with the lead. When you see the dog catch the body scent, ask for the find signal you have selected for disaster work: "Sit," "Speak," etc. Praise the dog instantly. Go to the subject and help him out of hiding. Both of you then praise the dog.

Repeat with the dog off-lead. Have the subject hidden in a different obstacle. Be ready to restrain the dog verbally on the "Check it out" command (grab his collar only if you must).

Finally, have the subject hide in the scary place at the end of the course. With your "Hunt--careful" command, send the dog ahead. Note his alert. You may want to give your "Check it out--careful" command, but do not go to the dog until he gives the speak or sit signal. If the entrance is securely blocked, the dog will try to signal you when he finds he can't get in. Then go to the dog, praising him and urging him to wait while you help the subject emerge (a firm "Wait!" or "Stay!" may be needed). Both of you should then praise the dog extravagantly.

Experienced dogs may pick this up very quickly. To keep them on their toes, you can turn this into a multiple-victim problem by locating one subject mid-course and another at the end.

THINGS TO THINK ABOUT

1. Having met all the obstacles previously in simpler form, does the dog remember and use the techniques he learned earlier to cross them? Most dogs will. If yours does not, return to simpler obstacles of the same type for one or two sessions.

2. Did the dog alert to the hidden subject at a reasonable distance, or was he so distracted by the obstacles that he only noticed the scent when right on top of it, if at all? Build up his confidence; then try again.

3. Does the scary-looking place inspire a cautious approach by the dog? That's what you want. Adding Halloween-type decorations may help.

4. In the multiple-victim case, does the dog respond immediately to your "Find another--careful" command? If so, try it again, but this time give no command. Pretend you are fully occupied helping the first victim to safety. Does the dog make the second find on his own? If he seems very sure of himself, proof him by asking, "Any more there? If not, come!" The dog should refuse to leave the area with another victim hidden close by. He should insist on making a reasonable check of the whole locale.

LESSON 3 -- PLACES WITH BAD FOOTING

Preparation. If your training site affords natural obstacles, use them. Some possibilities are a steep slope covered with ice or mud, a heap of rocks at the foot of a cliff, a stream bank with slippery logs to crawl over and under, sand dunes, gullies with unstable walls, a log jam or a mountain "blow-down," a creek bed or large drainage ditch soon after a flash flood. You may need to simulate these conditions with piles of boxes and junk, stacks of fence posts, a collection of shipping pallets laid every which way (the more unstable, the better). Our intent is to practice under conditions that might be found after an earthquake or a bad storm.

In this lesson, don't worry about having a variety of obstacles; try instead for one very large and difficult obstacle in each session. If the opportunity arises to work in a dust storm or torrential rain or blizzard, take advantage of it to the fullest extent that is safe.

Be sure to warn those who hide for your dog of the hazards. Select a spot where the dog cannot get to them readily. If they can imitate being pinned down by logs, hemmed in by rocks, or otherwise incapacitated, it will make the problem more realistic, but don't risk their actually being injured.

The course through the obstacle need not be lengthy. Crossing the site to the victim(s) should, however, be a challenge to the dog's courage and judgment, and threatening enough that he will urge you to be careful.

Working the course. When the subject(s) are in place, bring the dog to the edge of the site on lead. Release him with your "Hunt-- careful" command. Remain at the edge at least until the dog's first alert. Then enter the area cautiously. The dog must learn that in some conditions you cannot move as readily as he (while in others you can move better). He should wait close to the find until you discover or clear a safe way to him.

Make it easier for your dog to wait by giving verbal encouragement (unless a stream of chatter distracts him from what he is doing). In any case, do develop a verbal response to his speak or sit so that he knows you understand he has made a find and are coming as quickly as possible.

When you reach the victim, give the dog at least a little verbal praise before you begin extricating the victim. A disabled victim cannot praise the dog, so your approval is especially important. During the last session, mark the spot and remove the dog from the disaster zone. Let him watch someone else extricate the victim, assuring him all the time that his effort was worthwhile.

In subsequent attempts, vary the victim's hiding place. One time it can be close to where you start; another time, at the farthest point in the disaster zone. Use two or more victims. Let one disappear while you are bringing out the other, so that the dog must find the first victim twice.

THINGS TO THINK ABOUT

1. Does the dog seem able to apply what he learned on the obstacle courses to a more natural situation?

2. Does he search the difficult terrain independently, seeming to understand that you will join him if there is need of you; for instance, to administer first aid?

3. Are there signs that your dog is choosing a preferred route through the hazards? Is he thinking of you, or only of himself?

4. Does the dog register a good alert? A good find indication?

5. If there were ten incapacitated persons trapped in the search area, how many of them would the dog find? (This is the standard question with which the coordinator assesses your probability of detection--if you say, "Seven," then he enters "70%" on his map or chart.)

6. If someone managed to drag himself out of the wreckage and collapsed in a nearby ditch or thicket, would your dog detect him? Test this by placing a subject just outside your search area.

LESSON 4 - ARCHITECTURAL COLLAPSE

Preparation. If you can get permission to use it, an actual demolition site is ideal. Hint: most contractors can't give you permission because of their liability insurance, but on some large projects (highway renewal--and yes, the cleanup after a tornado or flood) those in charge won't object if you keep out of the workers' way (after hours, for instance)--or it may be that nobody has the authority to forbid you.

Be inventive. Sometimes a farmer has an old building he wants torn down and will let you practice in it first in exchange for your labor. A personal friend may be building or demolishing a structure. Or you can pile up wooden pallets, old boards, rusty pipes, shipping cartons, etc. Don't use anything heavy or sharp where it could fall and hurt someone. On light soil, you can give the structure a push and its collapse will produce a major scent obstacle--dust. Or you can throw a few buckets of dirt over the heap.

The structure should be large enough to have two or three "rooms" so that the dog will have to work out of sight and you can test the efficacy of his audible find signal (some handlers have the dog sit and listen for his tags to stop jingling). A hole or hollow in the center can simulate a basement.

Clutter up the approach with broken glass (or thistles, if you are afraid your dog will cut his pads), leaving a narrow zigzag path through it so the dog will learn to walk cautiously. You can form a bridge over the impediment out of stout boards supported on blocks. To save time, plan the structure with a different approach route for each team in your group and various hiding places for victims.

Working the course. Stand outside the area and remove the lead. Send the dog with your "Hunt--careful" command. In this small space, he may catch victim scent and alert before entering the area. Give the "Check it out--careful" command as soon as the dog alerts. You may want to add some verbal coaching and/or hand signals to help the dog find the "safe" path in the first try or so. What you want him to learn is that some paths are much preferable to others and he should look for the more desirable ones.

Your dog may sit or speak outside the room where the victim is hidden; he may be getting actual body scent. Go to him, cautiously, over the route he has selected, while giving verbal praise. Then send him on inside with a "Check it out--careful" command. Remain outside and listen closely. When you hear another find indication, go in carefully, praise the dog, and extricate the victim. Let the dog lead you out by the "safe" path.

On the second and subsequent tries, have two or more victims concealed. Be sure to carry your canteen. If your structure is challenging and you conscientiously added dust, your dog will need a drink after the first find. Watch him for signs of thirst (some dogs will scratch or sniff at your canteen or tin cup when their nasal passages start to dry out). Make a mental note of his preferred thirst signal so that you will recognize it under any circumstances.

You may remove the first victim before finding the second, or mark both and call for help in extricating them. In training, usually let the dog see the victims brought out, but occasionally end the session with just marking their location. In a real disaster, you will want to locate all survivors as soon as possible and will go on after you mark.

THINGS TO THINK ABOUT

1. Did the dog readily accept the need to choose a route and watch where he puts his feet? Did he do so efficiently? If not, go back to Lesson 2 and add some thistles or other penalties for stepping off the path.

2. Was the dog reluctant to enter the structure alone? Encourage him verbally, even looking in if you must. Do you still hear his find signal?

3. Did the dog appear concerned for the victims? If not, you must act more worried and they must act more distressed on subsequent tries.

4. When were signs of thirst evident? Did the dog's scenting ability appear to increase after a drink?

5. Have one victim leave a piece of clothing in the structure and crawl to a hiding place across the room. Does the dog alert on the clothing? Does he stand and air scent? If so, would he find this person faster by tracking?

6. When one victim remains to be found, ask the dog "All clear?" or "Shall we go home?" and start to leave. The dog should object. If he does not, heel him outside (off-lead), pretend to count victims and find one missing, then turn back and give a new "Hunt--careful" command. Does the dog grasp that he must not let you depart when a victim is still present?

LESSON 5 - VEHICLE DISASTERS

Preparation. Try to locate a wrecking yard or automobile dump for this problem, which simulates a train, plane, or multiple auto crash situation. Otherwise, have your tracklayers park their vehicles close together as if they have collided, lay down some metal siding and broken glass to hinder the approach, and simulate hydrocarbon odors with wads of cotton soaked in fuel, motor oil, antifreeze, etc. The cotton is easily picked up afterwards.

The victims should lie on the vehicle floors, jam themselves in behind cardboard boxes or shopping bags, or crawl underneath the vehicles. They should pretend to be unconscious. At first the doors should be left open; then just the windows; and finally all the doors and windows should be closed.

Later, have one victim leave a billfold or purse on the seat and crawl off as if injured to a place of concealment several paces downwind so the dog won't catch the scent before checking out the vehicle.

Have one victim construct a dummy by stuffing a shirt that has been worn during heavy exercise and attaching a cloth bag of hair combings for a head. A little blood from a pricked finger or spit on the dummy's head will make it more realistic scentwise. At first, put the dummy alone in the vehicle the dog will come to last when checking the accident scene (push it through the window with a pole from another vehicle to avoid having a live path of scent stronger than the dummy's that would lead the dog away). Later, drag the dummy with a rope downwind to a remote hiding place.

Working procedure. Bring the dog to the vicinity of the wreck, remove the lead, and give your "Hunt--careful" command. Watch for alerts, ready with a 'Check it out" command if appropriate, but prepared for a possible find signal not preceded by an alert because the vehicle disaster area is so small. At the find signal, go to the dog and praise him. Mark the location and send the dog on (a crash with only one victim is rare).

Next, find any victims that may have left scent objects in the vehicles but are hidden outside. Watch for signs of scent fatigue with all the hydrocarbon odors around. (Be ready with a firm "Leave it!" command if the dog starts to mouth anything you put out to hold the hydrocarbon odor; most of these substances are poisonous.) Give the dog a drink; and if he still shows signs of frustration or inability to work, move off for a few minutes to let him breathe fresh air and clear his nose. Note how long it takes him to recover.

When you start working with the dummy, the dog's signals may be very tentative, so keep a sharp eye out for them. Good timing of your verbal encouragement can turn confusion into certainty, and this is particularly important on the very first "body find." If the dog acts upset upon finding the dummy, call for the person who made the dummy to come running and reassure the dog. Otherwise, treat the dummy find like any other, marking the location and removing the dog with praise to make room for medical personnel and people more skilled than you at extricating accident victims.

Some report that their dogs will not approach or alert on a dead body. Therefore, we reassure the dog on his first contact with the dummy; he is less apt to avoid like objects in the future if he thinks miracles can occur. (Besides, sometimes they do!) Consider the reaction of the Bloodhound, Boomerang, (Brey/Reed, p. 121) who retreated in "distress and confusion" from his first encounter with a body, yet twice after that trailed directly to a body and had to be dragged away. Dogs are generally realists.

In the last session, one of those who has left a scent object in a vehicle should go at least a hundred paces before hiding. Try to get the dog to track the victim (use your verbal "Track it" command), unless you have trained him exclusively for air scent. Sometimes crash victims, stunned and disoriented, have staggered a mile or more before collapsing.

THINGS TO THINK ABOUT

1. Is the dog's approach properly cautious? If not, have a victim pop a balloon or bang two pieces of metal as the dog dashes up to the wreck.

2. Does the dog locate victims in the vehicle first, then those around or under it, and finally those who have wandered off? This is desirable: the ones pinned inside usually need help quickest. Encourage it.

3. The **second** time he finds a dummy, does the dog take it in stride? If not, produce another "miracle". (Should the dog pay absolutely no attention to the dummy, you need one with more realistic scent simulation. Don't worry about its looks; the dog doesn't.)

4. What are your observations of interference from the hydrocarbon smell? Does the dog adapt to it and discriminate against it? Could he track the victim out of the immediate area despite this interference?

LESSON 6 - THROUGH FIRE AND FLOOD

Preparation. Make every effort to set these up where there has been a real fire or flood. Our dogs have now learned techniques for most types of disaster, and it only remains to give them experience under the scenting conditions they must learn to screen out. A fire leaves a pervasive odor that could overwhelm a creature whose strongest response is to scent. As with the dank, rotten smell of flood debris, you and your dog must experience it and learn to work with it.

In the west, there are many acres burned over each year by forest, prairie, and brush fires. Road ditches and railway embankments are commonly cleared by fire. In spring and again in fall, weeds are usually burned off the banks of irrigation ditches. Farmers and gardeners sometimes burn over a field or two. Vacant lots in small towns may be burned off each autumn. Having found a burned area, use a rake to clear a narrow, zigzag approach. Set up some obstacles to conceal victims in the center. Dust ashes over everything. Create live coals by burning blocks of wood or pieces of charcoal; spot them along the sides of the approach. Don't worry about the dog's burning his feet--he'll detect the heat farther away than you would; and besides, he's been practicing with thistles and broken glass.

Run-off from melting snow creates spring floods all over the North and in mountainous areas. Heavy rains flood whole towns in the South and along the Gulf Coast. The Southwest has its summer flash floods. There are also lake beds being drained and river levels being adjusted by dams that result in the characteristic flood odor as well as piles of debris that can be used in setting up your problem. Have the victims hide in log jams or packing crates brought in to simulate the flotsam stranded when the waters subside. Some can be up in trees cut off from the bank by the flow. Use planks to form bridges over mud and pools of water.

Most fire victims are inert (passed out from smoke inhalation). Flood victims stranded in trees or on rocks are usually responsive. Those pinned in debris may be in either condition. Use a dummy sometimes, as in the vehicle problem. It can be hoisted into tree limbs, allowed to float downstream, etc. Put plenty of space between your victims. The flood or fire often scatters survivors over many square miles. Also, your dog should extend his search pattern after the narrow confines of the collapsed-building and vehicle-crash problems.

Working procedure. Take your dog to the edge of the area, remove the lead, and give the "Hunt--careful" command. Note how the dog enters the area, using verbal praise to reinforce his progress if he is at all unwilling to thread his way between the glowing coals or the mud puddles and soaked debris. He won't like the smell of either place.

Enter the area and go part way to the dog after his first alert, so that you are close enough to detect his find signal. Use the path he has indicated; it will be the safest one for you as well. Encourage him verbally to check out the scent. Mark the location of each find and proceed at once to the next--pretend there is a crew of medics and men with heavy equipment following. When you have found all the victims you know to be out there, plus the dummy, give your "That's all" signal and head for the car. The scope of this disaster is so large that both you and the dog must be willing to leave some of it for other teams.

THINGS TO THINK ABOUT

1. Did the dog overcome his initial distaste for the smell? Bolster his confidence that you never ask him to search where there is nothing to find?

2. Was the dog efficient in finding the safe path which you had cleared into the area to the vicinity of the hiding places?

3. Did the dog miss the first victim? Was he still adapting to the presence of conflicting scent? How long should you allow for the dog's nose to adjust, on entering this type of disaster area?

4. Did the dog work effectively despite the smell? How did his alert and find distances compare with those of which he is normally capable?

5. Did the dog show scent fatigue? Did a drink of water cure it? Perhaps it will in the burn problem, but it may not in the flood case. If you had to take the dog out of the tainted area, how long did you need to wait before he seemed willing to go back to work? How long could he work effectively before needing another break?

6. Is the dummy becoming just like any other find to the dog? (Be sure you are not cueing the dog to treat it differently by your actions .)

LESSON 7 - MORE SCENT INTERFERENCE

Preparation. Use all your ingenuity to find places with pervasive odors that will tax the dog's scenting ability. Some of those available are found in nature, like the sulfurous fumes of mineral springs--these are a good imitation of what emerge from some volcanoes. Most smelly environments, though, are man-made. So are plenty of disasters.

One good place available to almost everybody is a rural garbage dump. Most of these are full of humps and holes that serve as multiple hiding places, all sorts of odors, and items obnoxious to you that the dog may regard as great treasures until you remind him he is working.

Another place that constitutes a major scent obstacle is a cattle feedlot. While the owner wouldn't want you moving a dog through his livestock any more than you would want to get trampled, after the cows are shipped out the lot still smells bounteously. Try it for a tracking problem. The many corral sections and partitions form an admirable maze. The point here is for the dog to adapt to and work in spite of the scent, but for practical application, some places still have stampede victims.

Use of many locales requires that you know the management extremely well and can overcome insurance problems, but if you can get permission, all the following are good scent challenges: machine shops, factories (some even let off vast jets of steam or smoke), laboratories of various sorts, hospitals (not much chance) or veterinary facilities (possible). Most also have agility challenges such as metal stairways and ladders, ramps, platforms, swinging or revolving doors, metal compartments or bins through which little scent will diffuse. You are more apt to be allowed to work in such places if you request permission to do so in off hours where the only persons your dog will frighten are the night watchmen. You might offer to give the security force a hand but don't be upset if they refuse. It costs nothing to ask.

Working procedure. Take the dog into the new environment and heel him around a little before removing the lead and telling him to "Hunt--careful. " (Be sure you've exercised him first; the leg-lifting habit to claim his find may be all right outdoors but will be frowned on inside.) Try asking the dog if he is "Ready to search?" He may surprise you with a very clear answer.

Set up both tracking and air scent problems in your chosen environment. They need not be long, but should allow you to introduce the dog to the major difficulties he will face if he ever has to search a place like this.

Take the opportunity to do a little public-relations with the person who opened up the place for you. Most of those who have never worked a dog are amazed at what one with scent training can do, and of course they will be impressed at how flawlessly your canine partner behaves. Even those with some fear of dogs will relax when they see that your dog pays almost no attention to them, being intent on the search he expects to come. People are constantly astonished at how seriously the search dog takes his work.

THINGS TO THINK ABOUT

1. Did the dog give you a clear signal when he had assessed the prevailing scents of the place and was ready to work in it? How long did this process take?

2. Was the dog uneasy in this new environment? (He shouldn't be, after all we have put him through. Do some more work, wherever you can, until he is confident both indoors and outdoors.)

3. What kind of scent environments reduce the dog's working range and efficiency the most? Are they the same ones that smell the strongest to you?

4. Is your dog now apparently ready for all sorts of physical obstacles as well as scent environments?

5. Did working the dog in these places suggest any adaptation of your handling procedure for the various conditions? Was this something you might have anticipated if you had stopped to think longer before setting up your problem?

AKC TRACKING TEST
LESSON PLAN

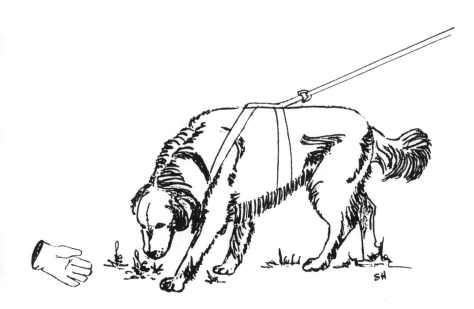

Starting stake.

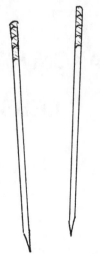

Crosstrack stakes.

Reflecting stakes for night work.

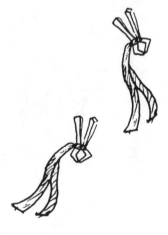

Clip-on trail markers.

Useful equipment for AKC tracking practice.

LESSON PLAN FOR AKC TRACKING TESTS

Objective. This lesson plan is designed for a single purpose, to get the dog that tracks "some" ready for the American Kennel Club Tracking Dog (TD) and Tracking Dog Excellent (TDX) tests. It will work both for those that have completed the TRACKING AND TRAILING Lesson Plan in this book and for those that have learned to track by other methods.

Why special instructions for passing these tests? What, exactly, do they contain?

The TD has two flags marking the start and initial line of travel, continues up to 500 yards with four or five turns (at least two at 90°), and ends with a glove. It is aged one-half to two hours. The dog's readiness must be certified by an AKC tracking judge before he can enter a TD test: thus, he must essentially pass the TD twice.

The TDX begins with a single flag beside an article scented by the tracklayer; the dog must choose the line of travel, negotiate 800 to 1000 yards with several turns (at least three at 90°), pass two obstacles (roads, fences), ignore crosstracks at two points, and find three articles (two dissimilar ones along the way, plus a glove or billfold at the end). The TDX track is aged three to five hours; the crosstracks are laid one to one and a half hours after the main track. One passing performance on the TDX earns the title; no certification is needed.

Neither test sounds too difficult. Results in the monthly AKC Awards publication, however, indicate some problems. In the 144 TD tests given in 1988, 502 dogs qualified out of 917 competing. In the 99 TDX tests given in 1988, only 73 qualified out of 429 competing. In over half those tests, **nobody** passed. Because two or three entries are submitted for every opening in the average TDX test and those who may actually compete are chosen by lot, you may wait years to get a second chance. Therefore, it pays to be sure of passing when you do get in. (Cut the odds by entering your national breed-club's tracking tests, which have fewer applicants because only dogs of a single breed are eligible.)

You can make your dog "fail-safe" on AKC tests by mastering one thing: he must work **only** the individual ground scent of the tracklayer.

The SAR dog, left to his own choice, will tend to use the trail scent re-emitted by moist objects along the track (judges may call it "tracking too wide") or else work from side to side of the cloud of lighter-than-air particles shed by the tracklayer (judges may call it "quartering"). He may work the day-old scent of a judge or committee member instead of the tracklayer's.

The dog that has practiced exclusively on very fresh tracks--aged a half-hour for the TD, aged three hours for the TDX--may be following the scent of disturbed earth and crushed vegetation. Such a scent path has only slight indications of directionality or age, and it tells nothing about who or what did the disturbing or crushing. Tracking disturbed earth and crushed vegetation will work reasonably well on the TD as long as the ground cover doesn't change to, say, bare gravel, though it requires the dog to "shift gears" to find the glove at the end. On the TDX, it may not even get the dog away from the starting stake in the right direction, and it gives scant clues to differentiate a turn from a crosstrack.

Fortunately, the cure for all these problems is the same. Start with a day-old track, then **decrease** the age while keeping the dog's attention on that individual ground scent. Oops, you've been told there is no individual ground scent after several hours? Test that theory for yourself. Try Lesson 1 of this outline. Does the dog track surprisingly well even though it's his first experience with a trail anywhere near this old? Just what was he tracking? It can't be crushed vegetation; the plant juices have sealed over the injury long since. It can't be disturbed earth; the wind has blown dust into the indentations, the raw mud left when a boot picked up the surface layer has dried out to form a new crust. What's left? Individual human scent.

We don't need to decide whether it comes from the slow diffusion back into the air of particles shed by the tracklayer or from bacterial action on these particles. All we need to know is that the scent is there. We can see the dog work it. When we add crosstracks, we observe that it is individualized. Now we get the dog to use it as his preferred source of information, no matter what other clues are present. That's what this lesson plan is designed to accomplish. After Lesson 5, most dogs are ready for TD certification. Continue through Lesson 7 to prepare for the TDX.

You should go through each exercise three times a week for two weeks. After each track, carefully appraise your dog's performance. Evaluate the influence of the weather occurring since the track was laid

Equipment Needed. The dog should have a nonrestrictive harness, as illustrated on page 42. You will need a 40-ft lead with some sort of marker at the 20-ft point. Lots and lots of scent articles articles are required--socks, shoes, T-shirts, caps, bandannas, billfolds, gloves of both fabric and leather. A portable mapping pad and pencil will help your tracklayer. Bring treats or a toy to help motivate the dog.

Through Lesson 5, you will need one tracklayer and two marker flags. The marker flags should be placed by someone other than the tracklayer, because in a real TD test the starting flags were probably placed by a judge or assistant and the only usable scent on them may be what settled there when the tracklayer passed by a foot or so away. Don't inadvertently teach the dog to assume the flags give off the scent he is supposed to follow. Don't worry about leather-soled footwear: the ground trail is formed by scent shed higher up falling into footprints, not seeping through the soles.

Ideally, use two additional people to lay crosstracks, although one walking the pattern twice will do (refer to the sketch in Lesson 6). You can lay both main and crosstracks yourself because of the time lapse, but using different people will give you more assurance. A dog that correctly tracks individual human scent may not need any crosstrack drill at all.

LESSON 1 - THE DAY-OLD TRACK

Preparation. Lay or have laid a five- or six-turn track about 500 paces long. The length of each leg should be somewhere between 80 and 200 paces. Place a scent article at the start, from two to four along each leg, and one at the finish of the track. (Use a scent article at the start even for TD practice; otherwise, unless tracks are visible in snow or mud, you can't be positive you are scenting the dog on the right person. We will add stakes in Lesson 2, and teach the dog to ignore them.)

Be sure the map includes definitive landmarks for the location of each leg and each turn. (Of course, all those articles will help!) Plan to run the track between 24 and 36 hours after it was laid. Do not put treats in the articles; over this time span, the resident wildlife would steal them.

Running the track. Walk your dog on lead to the first article, point to it and say, "Take scent." If necessary, pick up the article and tease him into sniffing it well. Unsnap your lead from the collar and fasten it to the D-ring of the harness. Point along the track and give your "Track it" command. (If you have been using "Track it" for SAR work, use a different command such as "Work close" for AKC practice.) Carry the scent article with you.

Follow the dog along the track, using tension on the lead to keep him from rushing frantically ahead but not so much as to discourage him. The many articles will help to control his pace, which should be brisk but steady. Gradually let out as much lead as you can keep taut; if it slacks, shorten up.

At the first article, praise and reward enthusiastically, then say, "Good dog, go find another one." If your dog has been working regulation TD tracks with no articles except the glove at the end, he may think that he's finished at the first find. Show no displeasure at this; simply re-scent him on the article he has just found and repeat, "Go find another one." After you do this once or twice, he should get the picture.

Note with care how closely the dog adheres to the track, especially at corners. If the dog starts to overrun an article or miss a corner, stop immediately and restrain him with the lead. Do not make leash corrections or verbal reprimands, but stand still and wait quietly until he notices what he missed; then and only then, run to him with praise and urge him forward.

Give vigorous praise for finding the last article, especially if your dog has been used in SAR and expects to find a person at the end of the track. Be sure your dog knows how delighted you are with his cleverness. Then give your "That's all" word or signal.

Comment. The preceding instructions may be unnecessary. Almost everybody who has been working fresh tracks is astonished at how well his dog does on an old one. The absence of air scent, the relative depletion of trail and ground-disturbance scent, and of course the many articles holding strong tracklayer scent combine to make this a very easy problem.

THINGS TO THINK ABOUT

1. Did the dog seem to keep his head down better and stay closer to the actual track than he may have on fresher ones? Once they realize there are many articles, most dogs tend to track closer to avoid missing some.

2. Did your dog seem more careful, especially on second and subsequent attempts? Could it be that on fresh tracks the dog thinks, "If I lose the track, I can always pick up the general direction from the air scent," whereas on old tracks the dog finds no air scent to switch to?

3. If track loss does occur, does the dog change his technique of trying to recover it? How? Is the new method more successful?

4. Does the dog's motivation seem to be increasing? Is he beginning to take pride in the find for its own sake rather than looking for a treat?

5. By the fifth try, has the dog formed a habit of preferring the ground scent? Does he show less frequent track loss and tendency to miss articles? Do you no longer need the "Work close" command?

LESSON 2 - TWELVE-HOUR TRACK WITH SCENT OBSTACLES

Preparation. Lay or have laid a five- or six-turn track as in Lesson 1, but increase the total length by making four or more of the legs at least 120 paces long. Continue to use many scent articles. Have someone other than the tracklayer put in a stake on the left side of the first article, about two feet away the first session, then progressively closer down to six inches. For TD practice, have a second stake placed about 30 paces down the track. Age tracks at least twelve hours, and run them at different times of day.

Plan the track to include both types of scent obstacle: a relative lack of scent (bare rock or pavement) and too much scent (pools). In this lesson, all tracks should go directly across the scent obstacles at the narrowest point. The level of difficulty should increase gradually. For example, a narrow path of bare dirt; a two-rut forest road; a strip of blacktop; a little-used two-lane paved road; a superhighway or shopping-mall parking lot closed for repair.

Similarly, start your scent pools with a small hollow; work up to a little clearing surrounded by thick brush; next, a sand pit or dry catch pond; then, a damp ditch or shallow puddle; finally, a running stream. At first, do not put an article within the pool--better to have one a few feet beyond the far edge, where the article's pool can leak into the obstacle pool and help the dog find the quickest way out. As the pools become larger and the dog learns how to handle them, do put articles in the pools.

Running the track. Start the dog as in Lesson 1. Try to reach and maintain a 20-foot working distance as required for AKC tests.

At each find, run to your dog so he doesn't have to retrace too long a path when he continues. Your praise must still be enthusiastic, but try to temper it so that the dog doesn't become too excited to proceed. You want him to feel rewarded, but ready and eager for the next task.

With the obstacles, likewise, try to interrupt the dog's forward progress as little as possible. The first one may be so slight that the dog will not even notice it. If loss of track should occur, stop and increase the lead tension while the dog works it out. At an interface between two ground conditions (for instance, where the track goes from grass to bare pavement), it may help to walk backward so that the dog approaches the interface again on a strong scent. Increase the lead tension. Let the dog check cracks and weeds growing in them if these are close to the direct line of travel, but do not let him range wide. Allow him to pick up the trail on the other side and reestablish his working distance before you cross.

Redouble your praise on the next find. The reward must match the effort if the obstacles are to enhance the dog's sense of achievement.

THINGS TO THINK ABOUT

1. Did the dog pay no attention to the flag(s), even when close to the article? Good! If he sniffs a flag, use your "Leave it" command, direct his attention again to the article, and start him off promptly. You want the dog to regard flags as totally irrelevant.

2. Is the dog aware by this time that, after a find, there's more to come? Does he give you the article almost impatiently and put his nose down again at once? This is desirable, but watch closely and don't let him skip articles.

3. Did the dog indicate confusion when the track crossed an interface, then in two or three paces recognize it as the same track despite its having a different odor on the new surface? Sometimes this recognition comes as abruptly as if a light had been switched on. If you see no recognition, encourage the dog to go forward in a straight line until he hits the strong, familiar scent on the other side, then praise him. Build up his faith that difficult conditions do not last. (And repeat this lesson, with variations, an extra week.)

4. On the bare surface, did the dog make use of scent trapped in cracks and small depressions? If he shows confusion or loss of track, you may need to point out some of these minute scent depositories to teach him that there is always something to be found, even if it is faint.

5. Did you see the dog's nose come up in the scent pool, followed by loss of track? Increase the tension, or even back up, until he recognizes that the ground trace offers a faint, continuous line through this confusing cloud of plentiful but directionless air scent?

LESSON 3 - MORE SCENT OBSTACLES

Preparation. Track should again have five or six turns and many articles, including one close to the stake at the start. The total length should be up to 1000 yards. Start out ageing tracks six hours and work down to three or four hours, running them from early morning to mid-day. The skill developed here comes slowly, so allow plenty of time for both dog and handler to work it out.

The first week, have the track cross the obstacle at an oblique angle. The tracklayer should place a trail marker where the track leaves the obstacle so that you can see up ahead the location of the strong continuing trail. The second week, have the track make a turn within an obstacle, or run along its edge to come out at a point far removed from "straight across." When the dog is handling this well, try having the track emerge on the same side as it entered but some distance up or down the boundary. Obstacles may now be extensive: a large rock outcrop or a wide marsh.

Running the track. Proceed as you have previously. Be sure to study the tracklayer's map carefully before you start so that you know precisely what to look for and can give timely reinforcement when the dog makes the right choice (although, as usual, you must avoid guiding him).

Few dogs will not have a track loss under these circumstances. Part of the handler's job is to assure the dog that the game isn't over when this occurs, and to teach him that the trail is recoverable.

One technique is to allow the dog enough line to proceed out of the obstacle and then search up and down the far edge (the near edge in the same-side problem), while you remain stationary until you see a track alert. Then go with your dog, giving verbal reassurance: "Good dog. You've got it! Now work close!" This method must be used when the judges put the TDX starting flag and article in a hollow conducive to forming a scent pool. Be warned: they frequently do this.

Another technique is to back up until the dog returns to the start of the obstacle, then take him on a short lead around its perimeter until you see the track alert. When the dog's nose drops, praise him and repeat your "Work close" command. In a same-side emergence, this method is more efficient than the other, but it may get you 50 yards off the track in an AKC test, thereby disqualifying your dog. So the first method is recommended for AKC tracking, especially since judges seldom lay out a track that exits a scent pool on the same side as it entered.

If your dog never has a track loss, you can contrive one (by having a closed vehicle transport the tracklayer 100 yards along a forest road, for example) in order to create the opportunity of teaching your dog recovery techniques. But if your sole aim is to pass AKC tests, this may be a waste of time because the situation may never arise where you will need them.

All handlers should practice running tracks between mid-morning and mid-afternoon. When the net energy flow is **into** the earth, scent also goes down into the ground, and when the air just above the earth heats, its rise carries the scent aloft, leaving very faint traces on the surface. Unfortunately, the latter time is when most of the dogs in a test must run. Under these conditions, only the close-tracking dog has a real chance of success, and slow, careful dogs have a great advantage. If your dog's natural style is fast and flashy, you can moderate it with tension on the lead. But take care: don't destroy his desire to track.

THINGS TO THINK ABOUT

1.   Does your dog's manner change as he enters a scent pool or obstacle? Would you recognize the signs in a real test, with no map?

2.   Are you becoming alert to the presence of scent obstacles when you look over a course with your tracklayer? When you run the track, does your dog's performance show that your assessment was correct?

3.   Is the dog fully aware that the track is the same although it smells different in various ground covers? If not, lay out tracks crossing interface after interface, so close together that he can't "get set" between them.

4.   Are your dog's track loss and track recovery signals clear to you? (It may be an advantage if these signs are not equally clear to the judges and onlookers, so don't try to amplify them as long as you can read them.)

5.   What is your dog's instinctive approach to track recovery? Is it effective? Would it "pass" with AKC judges: does it look like the dog is clearly working at all times, and is the track recovered within 50 yards?

LESSON 4 - PHYSICAL OBSTACLES

Preparation. Have the track laid in irregular terrain where you are apt to encounter the "gullies, plowed land, woods, vegetation of any density...streams, hedgerows, fences, bridges..." that the AKC specifies. Seek to present the dog with progressively more challenging physical obstacles: a low wall, followed by a barbed-wire fence, then by a chain-link or woven-wire barrier with a gate. Age these tracks one to two hours.

Do advise your tracklayer not to use places a human can climb with fingers and toes where a dog cannot follow. AKC judges never make it that difficult. Otherwise, he can utilize all the obstacles your terrain has to offer.

Now ask your tracklayer to make sure each track contains at least three right-angle turns. Two or more are required in the TD and three or more in the TDX, not because of any difficulty inherent in 90° but rather so the judges can see how your dog works different wind directions. Besides, your dog makes a big impression if he runs such nice, square corners that onlookers can trace the track pattern on the ground just by watching him.

With so much going on to hold the dog's attention, this is also a good time to have two people with clipboards walk some 50 or 100 paces behind the handler, simulating the two judges. At first, they should keep silent; later, they should chat to present a progressively greater distraction.

Running the track. Physical obstacles involve only one new problem for the dog: learning to wait while you get yourself up or down a slope, open a gate for him, untangle the lead from bushes, etc. If you have not already taught a "Wait up" command, do so now (see p. 52, question 5).

In thick brush or forest, be ready to drop the lead. Walk around the obstacle and pick up the lead smoothly on the other side. If it gets caught, take hold of it and drag it clear (be careful not to get thistles or cactus thorns in your hand). The lead seldom gets hung up when the dog moves straight ahead, but it often happens if he circles. Therefore, encourage your dog to work forward at a uniform pace.

You should also drop the lead when the dog runs up or down a steep slope where you need your hands to climb. If you try to hang on, you may lose your footing and either fall on your dog or pull him off a ledge with you. If the dog gets too far ahead, use your "Wait up" command. The dog should sit on the next fairly level spot until you arrive at the end of the lead. Pick it up smoothly and continue.

As you approach a barbed-wire fence, shorten the lead so that the dog can't range along it; tell him "Wait up." Put your foot on the bottom wire and hold the others up while you encourage the dog to crawl through; then make him wait for you. After your release word, he should reach working distance before you follow. Letting him through a gate is handled similarly.

Most dogs will track straight on across bridges and through culverts, but some need lots of reassurance. If such an obstacle stops your dog, practice that type of obstacle in isolation. Get him to retrieve through it. When he traverses the obstacle alone and returns with his retrieve object, you can reintroduce it in a track. Just as with a thicket or a steep slope, drop the lead when the dog enters the culvert and pick it up again after he comes out the far end.

Don't make too much of the obstacles. The dog should regard them as normal occurrences or, at most, minor delays. If the dog has no problem with a particular obstacle, don't spoil things by calling it to his attention. This "all in the day's work" attitude is what you are striving for.

THINGS TO THINK ABOUT

1. Do you agree that, in general, physical obstacles affect the handler more than the dog?

2. After you have helped the dog through a fence or gate a time or two, does he understand that he should wait for your aid and then for you to get through?

3. Can you drop the lead and recapture it smoothly on the other side of an obstacle? If it gets snagged, does the dog wait quietly while you free it? These techniques help the TD handler stay calm and confident.

4. Does the dog track wide or quarter due to the freshness of the trail? Control his deviation with lead tension. Hold him in close on 90° turns.

5. Is the dog distracted by having people behind him? Use verbal encouragement to keep his mind on his work until he learns to ignore them.

LESSON 5 - MIXED OBSTACLES, FRESH TRACK

Preparation. Plan the tracks to include both scent pools and barriers, at least two physical obstacles, three or more 90° turns, and only two scent objects besides those at the start and finish. Put the scent objects on track legs that do not contain obstacles. Let the length of leg vary from 60 to 250 paces. Age these tracks from a half hour up to two hours (let the tracklayer tell you how old they were after you run them). Incidentally, the age of the track is measured from the time the tracklayer starts laying it to the time that the dog and handler start running it.

Again, get two people to walk behind you as you handle, simulating the judges. Have them talk to each other a lot, and even occasionally address some remarks to you. At least once, let the tracklayer be one of these people; if possible, let the two "judges" walk with the tracklayer a time or two as he lays out the track. In a real AKC test, the judges' scent (a day or so old) will be on the track as well as the tracklayer's, so the dog must learn to ignore air scent behind him while he works even if the same persons' scents are present on the track he is trying to follow.

Running the track. Because this lesson is in the nature of a review and puts together all you have previously learned, work especially on your handling skill. Try to keep the dog out at least 20 feet ahead of you between obstacles, turns, and articles. If your dog will work comfortably closer to 40 feet than 20 feet ahead, that's the safest habit to develop.

Some judges consider it very bad form to talk too much to your dog (although the AKC rule book states that only "guiding the dog" is cause for failure), so minimize your verbal encouragement. A judge who is impressed with your dog's total independence may give you the benefit of the doubt in a questionable situation, but one who feels you were on the edge of overhandling from the start will not hesitate to disqualify you. Recognize when the dog really **needs** a word from you and apply it promptly; otherwise, remain quiet, calm, and watchful, and merely follow along.

Be critical of your lead handling. Avoid anything that may even look like correcting or giving direction to your dog. If you hold the lead high, above your head, you can keep it free from entanglement with less tension. Remember, you may **restrain** the dog (even to backing up) but you may not **guide** him.

When loss of track occurs (and it can, even in the TD), don't panic. There is no time limit on the dog as long as he appears to be actively searching for the track. Lifting the head to air scent for it, though, sometimes causes a judge to say the dog has stopped tracking. If the dog actually does recover the track by air scent but manages to do so with his nose quite close to the ground, it probably won't count against him. A little judicious tension on the lead may keep his head down, and verbal encouragement can keep him moving. Above all, avoid telegraphing a sense of desperation to the dog. Passing may be very important to you, but your dog will recover the track more efficiently if you can repress that feeling and focus on the practical aspects of not impeding the dog's work.

Some very successful tracking handlers say that you should scan the horizon for obvious landmarks the judges may have used in laying out the track. I advise against it. A landmark that looks obvious to you on the track may not even have been visible to the judges at the start of the leg; and if you have no preconceived idea of where the track lies, you won't subconsciously guide your dog. Hunting for landmarks also distracts you from the more useful task of reading your dog so you know exactly where he loses scent, thus how far you should back up to help him regain it.

THINGS TO THINK ABOUT

1. Does the dog keep his nose down close upon the ground scent even though these tracks are so recent that fresh air scent is almost surely present? If not, run two or three tracks aged at least overnight, then try a fresh one again.

2. Is the dog working confidently out toward the end of the lead? If not, reassure him with some obstacle-free tracks having only two or three legs.

3. Did the dog seem to get bored or careless with fewer articles to find, or were the obstacles a sufficient challenge to hold his interest?

4. Does having the tracklayer walk behind you distract the dog? Ask him to start far, far back and gradually move up to about 30 paces. If the dog loops back to check out the tracklayer, command "Leave it!"

5. Did loss of track occur? Did the dog make a successful recovery?

6. Reread the AKC rules. How does your handling measure up? Are you doing or saying anything that might be misunderstood by a judge?

LESSON 6 - INTRODUCTION TO CROSS TRACKS

Preparation. Have a 600- to 1000-pace track laid on average tracking terrain with a wide, flat place where flags can be seen for a good distance. At two points where the track loops around on this flat (preferably not on adjoining legs), have the tracklayer thrust a stake into the ground with each hand. After the track has aged from one to one and a half hours, have the crosstrack-layers enter the flat place and walk abreast, about four feet apart, so that one passes on each side of the line defined by the stakes. They should keep the stakes lined up as they approach.

One crosstrack-layer can do the job if he walks across the flat keeping the stakes about two feet to his right side, then pivots around and walks back, again keeping the stakes about two feet to his right as he returns. The diagram below shows the results: two parallel tracks, four feet apart, intersecting the main track perpendicularly at two points, just as in the two person case.

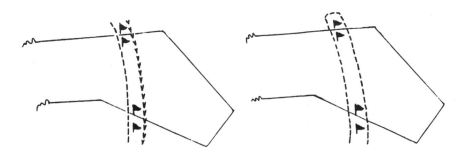

Two crosstrack-layers   One crosstrack-layer

At first, have the crosstrack-layers leave the stakes in so you will know where to look for the dog's reaction. Later, have them pull the stakes out and carry them off the course. The main track should be aged a total of three hours.

Running the track. Start off just like any other track. When you see the stakes coming up, note carefully the dog's reaction. Let him take his time if he wishes--this is a new situation for him. He may sniff both ways at each crosstrack, or even take several steps. Restrain him with the lead, however, if he starts actually to follow a crosstrack (you are allowed up to 50 paces, but don't push it). Give your "Leave it" command. Stand where you are and hold fast until the dog swings around over the true track again.

Chances are his nose will go down or he will switch directions abruptly and start off the way he sould go. Give verbal praise and slack off the tension. Let the dog get out at least 20 paces before you follow.

Your dog may charge right between the stakes as if they weren't there and no crosstracks existed. If this happens, don't fight it--rejoice and go look through the AKC Events Calendar for upcoming TDX tests.

THINGS TO THINK ABOUT

1. Does the dog alert on the first crosstrack? Does he also alert on the other? Is this a different kind of alert than for an article or for track recovery?

2. After the first few tries, when you no longer have stakes to go by, can you tell from the dog's behavior where the crosstracks were (look for the holes where the stakes were pulled up)? If you can, be sure to praise the dog when he has passed each intersection safely. (If your answers to both 1 and 2 are "no", skip to 5.)

3. Is your dog's manner in taking a crosstrack distinct from the way he rounds a corner? Enough so that you would feel secure restraining him on an unmarked crosstrack in a test? When you restrain him and say, "Leave it," does he return to the main track willingly, even gratefully?

4. If your dog gives a clear alert, then starts to turn about four feet farther on, what is probably happening? What would you do about it? If you had a classic 90° turn 30 to 50 paces back and your dog starts another 90° turn, would you allow it, or would you stop and restrain him? Why?

5. Did your dog show absolutely no signs of noticing a crosstrack? Then you have no need to worry about any extraneous track that crosses the one you are running. Skip Lesson 7--you don't need it.

LESSON 7 - PROOFING ON CROSSTRACKS

Preparation. Ask that the main track and crosstracks be laid as in Lesson 6. However, as the crosstrack-layers approach each pair of stakes, they should test the wind, and one should drop an article bearing his scent 20 paces before or after crossing the main track, depending on the wind direction. (Distraction articles are always placed so that the wind carries their scent across the main trail, assuring that the dog will detect them.)

It will help you if the distraction articles are some color such as blaze orange, which is very noticeable to a human but is seen as a dull brown (if at all) by the dog. Both pairs of stakes can be pulled out; an obvious article off the track is enough clue to the handler of the crosstracks' presence.

Running the track. You will probably see the article long before you get to the crosstrack location--a color anomaly is as obvious to you as movement is to the dog. Be ready as you approach the point where a line from the article intersects your path perpendicularly. If your dog air scents the distraction article and alerts in its direction but then drops his nose to the main track and continues on his way (the most probable case), you need do nothing. Run another practice track or two, just to make sure, and then start sending off TDX entries.

If your dog starts along the crosstrack toward the article or, worse yet, leaves the main trail before he gets to the crosstrack and starts for the article on an angle, give a firm "No! Leave it!" command and stop dead, applying a strong restraint to the lead. The dog will tend to swing back toward the main trail. When he crosses it and shows his track alert, relax the tension on the lead and go with him, giving verbal praise. Continue to run tracks in this mode until the dog stops trying to leave the true path when a distraction article is present--if this requires much repetition, mix in some tracks stressing different problems so that your dog doesn't get bored.

If your dog really persists in wanting to retrieve the distraction article (as he may, should you be unready and fail to stop him before he gets it in his mouth), run this exercise two or three times with the distraction article made less attractive by the use of cayenne pepper or Bitter Apple™. Then let him reach it and he will most likely decide you were right in maintaining this was not an article he ought to pick up. As an alternative, the crosstrack-layer could put a set mousetrap or a balloon on top of it. Do whatever you must to convince the dog that only articles bearing the odor he was scented on are desirable.

This exercise is useful not only for assuring yourself the dog will not take a crosstrack but also for avoiding the dog's picking up articles other than the ones dropped by the main tracklayer. Picnickers or casual hikers may have discarded something along the track, coincidentally, either before or after your track was laid. It is not unknown for a judge to drop a handkerchief or a pencil in the process of laying out the track, and I once failed a TDX when my dog found a screwdriver belonging to a man who had been assisting the judges during layout.

THINGS TO THINK ABOUT

1. Is your dog more drawn to the distraction article than he was to the plain crosstracks? Why?

2. Does your dog stop opposite the distraction article and alert, then return to his work without taking so much as one step off the track? This is the ideal reaction; give lots of praise.

3. If your dog goes toward the distraction article, does he readily return to the main track on your "Leave it" command? That is good. A few more tries and your dog should stop being attracted by articles with the wrong scent. Some dogs get the idea much more quickly than others, of course. If your dog was force-broken to retrieve, practic and patience may be needed to override his compulsion to grab any article that comes within his reach.

4. Run a track with crosstracks at two points but no distraction articles. Do you read your dog more clearly now, and feel greater confidence than previously that your dog is not going to take a crosstrack?

BIBLIOGRAPHY

Following are a number of publications containing supplementary information dog handlers may wish to examine. I have tried to indicate for which area of training each has the most application.

Tracking Regulations, American Kennel Club.5580 Centerview Drive, Suite 200, Raleigh, NC 27606-3390 (September 1, 1995). When ordering, request "latest edition" as this publication is reissued frequently.

Rules and guidelines for AKC tracking, essential in preparing for AKC tests. Contains specifications for the newVariable Surface Tracking (VST) test as well as for the familiar Tracking Dog (TD) and Tracking Dog Excellent (TDX) tests. Those preparing for urban search work may find the VST requirements of special interest.

Catherine F. Brey and Lena F. Reed, **The Complete Bloodhound,** Howell Book House, Inc., New York, NY (1978).

Primarily a breed book, but accounts of individual dog and handler achievements are helplful in delineating what dogs can do. Contains a bfief summary of how to start a trailing dog.

Wentworth Brown, **Bring Your Nose Over Here,** ASAP Press, Albuquerque, NM (March 1992). Republished by the Weimaraner Club of Northern Illinois in September 1994, and currently available from WCNI, 6971 North Tonty Avenue, Chicago, Illinois 60646 ($5.00).

Excellent training guide for AKC tracking. Some "problem solving" techniques are applicable to trailing and air scenting, but these topics are not addressed specifically.

Sandy Bryson, **Search Dog Training,** The Boxwood Press, 183 Ocean View Blvd, Pacific Grove, CA 93950 (1984).

Vivid accounts of actual searches, much useful background infor-mation. Emphasis is on air scent and on the total search dog.

Major L. Wilson Davis, **Go Find! Training Your Dog to Track,** Howell Book House, Inc.. New York, NY (1974).

Best of the older books on tracking, good background information. Very little on air scent or trailing.

Glen R. Johnson, **Tracking Dog Theory & Method,** Arner Publi-cations, Inc., Rome, NY (1975).

Much used as an AKC tracking maual, especially in the East. Theory should be tested against handler's field observations before it is applied. Obedience slant is evident.

Colonel Konrad Most, **Training Dogs: A Manual** (translated from the German by James Cleugh), Popular Dogs Publishing Co., Ltd, 3 Fitzrooy Square, London WI (12th edition published in Germany 1951, 10th impression in Great Britain February 1972--first written in 1910).

Recognized as standard work on dog training throughout Europe. Covers all types of dog training. Though much has been learned since, many insights are still valuable for scent work. Compare with volumes by later writers who "went on" from Most, noting subtle shifts of emphasis. Original deserves to be taken literally.

National Police Bloodhound Association, Inc., **Police Pocket Training Manual for Bloodhound Handlers,** G. Malcolm Deiser, Lyndon Press, Louisville, KY (Ed. 1, 1977).

How to start trailing hounds (little application to tracking or air scent). The beginner may need a personal mentor to interpret or amplify.

Milo D. Pearsall and Hugo Verbruggen, M.D., **SCENT: Training to Track, Search, and Rescue,** Alpine Publications, Inc., Loveland, CO (1982).

Particularly good discussion of how a dog's senses actually work in early chapters. Pearsall's "Search and Tracking Match" is formulated in the spirit of AKC tracking, not as a test of scenting capability. Contains valuable training pointers, but heavily oriented towards Obedience.

William G. Syrotuck, **Scent and the Scenting Dog,** Arner Publications, Inc., Clark Mills, NY (3rd printing, 1980).

Syrotuck pioneered the use of dogs for search work in the eastern United States. His focus was on air scent. Of his many publications, this one contains the most information directly useful to the search dog trainer. His statistical approach to defining probable search areas is worth study, but the dog handler who attends SAR seminars will get all he can use verbally, with computer applications.

ABOUT THE AUTHOR

Of all training activities, author Lue Button finds scent work the most satisfying, as it calls for the highest development of canine skill and fosters the closest relationship between dog and handler.

Born in Fargo, North Dakota, Button trained animals on her grandparents' farm and went on to study anthropology, speech, and physics, earning her M.S. degree in Physics from the University of New Mexico in 1974. She has been employed by the Field Test Division at Los Alamos National Laboratory since 1968, retiring in January 1990. Upon her marriage to Donald Button in 1971, she became chief trainer for Von Knopf Weimaraners, studying tracking with Walter Bush and later Wentworth Brown in Albuquerque.

After a pivotal search mission with her tracking dog in 1982, Lue Button extended her dogs' training into all forms of scent work. She has taught numerous courses in obedience and tracking, and is currently training director of the Los Alamos-based Mountain Canine Corps.